A Bouquet of Wild Strawberries

Margarete (Gretl) Stockhammer Vegvari

Copyright© 2006 by Margaret Gretl Vegvari

All rights reserved. No part of this book shall be reproduced or transmitted in any form or by any means, electronic, mechanical, magnetic, photographic including photocopying, recording or by any information storage and retrieval system, without prior written permission of the publisher. No patent liability is assumed with respect to the use of the information contained herein. Although every precaution has been taken in the preparation of this book, the publisher and author assume no responsibility for errors or omissions. Neither is any liability assumed for damages resulting from the use of the information contained herein.

ISBN 978-0-7414-3622-1

Published by:

1094 New DeHaven Street, Suite 100
West Conshohocken, PA 19428-2713
Info@buybooksontheweb.com
www.buybooksontheweb.com
Toll-free (877) BUY BOOK
Local Phone (610) 941-9999
Fax (610) 941-9959

Printed in the United States of America
Printed on Recycled Paper
Published October 2006

This Book is Dedicated
to My Mother
Theresia Stockhammer

These Stories were
Lovingly Written

for My Children
Ilona and Ted

My Grandchildren
Michele and Adam

My Great-grandchildren
Max, Samantha
Nathan and Macy

and My Family in Austria

Eight Life-changing Events

1. Daddy's Girl – Losing My Father 1
2. Anschluss (Annexation) Austria/Germany
   As Seen Through the Eyes of a 15-Year-old Girl 7
3. WWII and the Impact on Our Family 13
4. Leaving Austria – Saying Goodbye to My Homeland 31
5. Start in Argentina and Living There 39
6. Leaving Argentina – To the Dominican Republic 49
7. To the USA – The Final Destination 65
8. Our Last Sunset 75

Short Stories

- Austria 87
- Hungary 111
- Argentina 119
- Santo Domingo (Dominican Republic) 133
- USA 141

Let Me Talk About My Mother 146
Looking Back On My Writing 150
A Letter To My Children 152

Margarete Stockhammer Vegvari, 2005 Torrance, California

LOOKING BACK....

When the number '80' in your life is telling you that the number left ahead of you is probably less than the fingers on your hands, your memory is a cherished gift.

I thought, what would be if somebody would ask me to write about the events in my life that had the biggest impact. You know, that brings it down to a compact size, leaving everything in between unsaid. But less boring, I think.

So, with that in mind, I will let my memory guide me along way back to my first... number one.

1
DADDY'S GIRL

LOSING MY FATHER

My father, Heinrich Stockhammer

Me, Gretl, age five

Daddy's Girl

LOSING MY FATHER

1927

The images of my father are as vivid today as they were 78 years ago. Not quite four years old, I see him coming home from work for lunch with his hat on, bending down on one knee to me, taking my hand and saying, "Come on, turn the hat around." And there it was, a bouquet of wild strawberries tucked in his hatband like a little flower bouquet. This is my earliest memory, it was the summer of 1926, it was his last summer to be.

A few months later I found myself sitting by his bed and he was asking me to sing for him, and with him. He was himself a wonderful singer and belonged to the Edelweiss Men's Choir. But his voice was letting him down, and tuberculosis took his breath away.

My father came back from Russia with tuberculosis. He was a proud man and did not want to admit he was sick. No one knew, because he made my mother promise not to tell anyone. When his boss and engineer co-workers came to visit, he was already too weak to walk around, but for them he put on a happy face and told jokes, so that when they left they said, "I don't know why they say he is deathly sick, he does not look so bad as they said." After they left, he collapsed in a sweat and he vomited a lot of blood. Mom had to take the bedpan filled with blood downstairs to the bathroom, which we shared with the owners, with instructions not to be seen by anyone. This was three days before he died. He had tuberculosis for six years.

He lived to see his last child who was born 17 days before his death. It was my youngest sister, Trude. I was told later, my mother gave birth on January 31, 1927, in the evening, in the next room, and was up the morning after to take care of her deathly ill husband. He would not let anybody take care of him but her. When the doctor came the next morning to check on him, he heard a baby cry and saw my mother attending my father. He could not believe what he saw.

My sister's birth happened soon after I was taken away from home to stay with my father's parents, the danger was too great for me to be infected. My youngest sister was 17 days old, my brother was five and a half, and my oldest sister was 12 years old. For the last four months they were taken care of by my mother's parents, as the exposure to my father's tuberculosis was dangerous. The reason I went to my father's family was because I was always considered to be more like his side of the family. I had a special bond with him, I was his little girl. When he was feeling very bad, he always asked me to sing for him. He would not allow me to be taken away from him. He always said, "When you take Gretl away then I know I am dying." That is why he was fighting with all his fading strength not to let them take me from him. But the day came, and I remember screaming as they took me from him, when they came for me.

My grandparent's house was an old farmhouse with a dirt road leading up between fields. It was an old cozy house with the typical European kitchen where the dining area is a corner bench and table by windows, I can still see the cross hanging in the corner. I was sitting there, looking out and seeing my father's brother, Uncle Toni on his bike coming uphill on the path. When he came in the house my grandmother and grandfather knew he had something important to say. The first words out of his mouth were 'Heinrich died today'. Nobody was paying attention to the little girl sitting there who understood, only when they heard me cry out.

As it was the custom at this time, the deceased was laid out at home. A lot of friends and acquaintances came to show their respect. Our house was filled with people who loved him, from his job and from the choir. Again, nobody paid attention when I came in this room. In all the commotion, nobody noticed me until they heard me scream as I was trying to touch my father. The bed was so high that I could only reach and touch his hand. The shock was so great for me that it took months for me to stop crying and asking for him. He was everything to me. I can only now imagine what that meant for my mother. I made her life even harder, and hard it was.

My father, back row, center. May 1916, a *lazaret* in Kremsmünster, Austria.

2

ANSCHLUSS (ANNEXATION) AUSTRIA / GERMANY

AS SEEN THROUGH THE EYES OF A 15-YEAR-OLD GIRL

My sister Trude (12) and I (16) in the garden below our house

ANSCHLUSS (ANNEXATION)

AS SEEN THROUGH THE EYES OF A 15-YEAR-OLD GIRL

1938

As I said when I started writing the first story, I will just skip the years and bring to life the things that formed and changed my life.

I am 15 years old now, working since I was 14 to help my mother out to feed three children. My oldest sister, Resi, now 22 years old, got married at 19, that left my mother to take care of Max, Trude, and me. That was more than she could do. I saw her many times filling our plates, putting them in the oven to keep the food warm….opening the oven, and counting the portions, one, two, three…shaking her head quietly, and going off to work without having eaten. Around the corner her mother would many times be waiting for her with a piece of bread and butter, saying, "You didn't eat again, did you?" So many times there was just not enough, but she made sure that we had what we needed.

It is 1938 and I see the Austrian flags being exchanged with the German swastika flag, it is almost not comprehensible. The people were told Adolf Hitler is coming to the city. So people lined the streets, curiosity took over to see the man who was changing their country. The people here waiting curiously now are the same people who were lining the streets just the day before waving the Austrian flag to support their Austrian

President in standing up against Germany. Nobody knew he had been forced to resign to avoid an unwinnable conflict. That was my first lesson in politics.

Of course, Hitler never came. After hour-long waiting, the German soldiers came marching through the streets, thinking all these people came to greet them.

Well, it was a brilliant propaganda trick, and it worked. The world would see that Austrians had made their choice, it looked that way to the outside world. Only the ones who had been there knew the truth. A few weeks later an election was held. I went with my mother to see it. There were no booths. In front of a long table was a committee of about four to five men. They handed my mother a pencil and a piece of paper to mark the "Yes" vote. Nobody in their right mind asked for privacy, or marked "No". One man did do it, he was not working in the factory the next day anymore. That was how Hitler got 99% of the Austrian votes.

Things changed rapidly. The working conditions at the textile factory improved dramatically for the better. The air quality, which was very bad, was rectified. The young workers like me at the age from 14 to 18 years were now only permitted to work 40 hours a week instead of 48. Fresh air was let in, and wooden planks were laid so we no longer walked or stood in water and in wet shoes. So there were improvements made for all workers, and that was gladly accepted.

But Austria was losing the character of the trusting old way, as one had to watch every word that might could get you in trouble. You never knew who is a party member, in other words, the freedom to speak out was gone.

So we were now part of Germany with the good and the bad things. Well, the future will tell us and give us the answer. And it sure told us, as we found out.

Resting along the Traun River (1941)

Trude (15) and I (19)

My brother Max (19) and I (17)

Max's soccer team. Max (18 or 19)
standing on far right.

Who needs boys? Trude, top row, second from right.
I am in front row center, to the right of the 'boy' holding flowers.

3

WWII

AND THE IMPACT ON OUR FAMILY

WWII Memorial in Gmunden

Max's name is five rows up from 1945.

WWII

AND THE IMPACT ON OUR FAMILY

1943

1943 Max was home on leave

We are now deep in WWII. Members of my family, uncles, cousins, and my brother are either in Russia or in France, fighting all against their beliefs in countries whose existence they only learned about in school. They never came home, and we never found out where they found their final resting place. In August of 1944, my brother Max was one of them. My mother's religious belief was tested, and God must have had a lot of patience, to listen to all the mothers of many of my closest friends. Too many sons are in places we will never know.

It is the fourth year of the war with Russia, and by the reports we are getting over the radio, we could tell that our soldiers are on the retreat. Offense has changed to defense. My brother was wounded in Russia in 1943, near Kiev. A bullet that missed his lung by about half an inch brought him home to recuperate. After about six months of hospitalization and rehabilitation, his hopes were so high that he now would not be sent back to Russia. On the day he got his orders, his hope was crushed, and Russia, again, was his destination. I remember when I walked him to the train station, how frightened he was. He said, "I was so hoping they send me to the West Front. I don't want to go back to that same place again." But for our mother he put on a brave face, saying, "The war will be over soon, mom, so don't worry." And so we said goodbye again. By then it was the beginning of August 1944, the Russian Army was on the offense and our soldiers were retreating from Russia. We never got a letter from Max, and we didn't know that two weeks after he left us, shrapnel from a grenade ended his young life. All the details came later, with a knock on our mother's door. The official notice by a party member was given to our mother.

The day when it happened was such an ordinary day. Trude had to go for her final exam to the Trade School in Linz, the capital of Upper Austria (Ober Österreich). Not to let her go alone, since it was a 68 km train ride to the city, I went with her.

It was a wonderful day, she passed the exam, we saw a movie, a comedy, and it was late afternoon when we came home. We lived in a three-story apartment building, my married sister Resi and her husband occupied the apartment on the first floor, we had ours on the third floor. It was very natural that we stopped in Resi's place first, thinking mom is probably there, as she so very often is. In her apartment, next to the wood-burning stove was a wooden coal box, this was mom's favorite place to sit, it almost belonged to her. This is where I found my mother. I never, as long as I live, will forget the face that made me stop my next step. White as a sheet, with eyes so red, was my mother's face. I looked at Resi and Ferdinand, and all I saw was eyes, as they look when they are out of tears. I don't remember what I said, or what Trude said, but one of the four of us said the name Max. I don't know much after this, I was with the rest of the family in a 'NO, I don't believe it, NOT Max' state of mind.

It was late at night when we had to think what has to be done. Resi said to me, "Tomorrow we have to make the arrangements for the service. Gretl, please take care of announcement that has to be printed." Nobody slept that night, and there I was, with that heavy task of getting Max's picture, gathering the dates, and putting together the announcement. But my feelings took over first, and I sat down with a pencil and emptied what was in my heart. I never wrote a poem before in my life, but something inside me let me find the right words. I did not have to look for them, they were just there for the writing, I did not have to think them.

The next few weeks, or was it months, mother was looking for God's answer to her question, WHY? It was an answer she never found. She stayed away from the little chapel in the Kinderheim where we all went every Sunday. Many weeks later, the priest came to visit her, and slowly, I think she made peace with God. But the hurt of a lost child, in a mother's heart, never stops.

MAX STOCKHAMMER

The poem I wrote for the Death Announcement
for my brother Max

When last you reached for our hands and left us
And with heavy steps walked through our door
Our hearts were filled with fear and anguish
And hope, that you would bring your young life back to us.

But in your book of destiny 'twas written,
You'd give your life for country and for us
In a battlefield in a distant land, remaining
And never feel again your mother's touch.

Our mother raised you under heavy hardship
to the young man you have become since father died
You were her pride you gave her your protection
and now we heard - you fell - you died.

When night falls and the stars shine brightly
There will be one we'll recognize as true
from now forever, will we search the heavens
the one that shines the brightest must be you.

1945

As the war came to an end, and the occupation began, we saw American soldiers everywhere. The occupation of Austria was divided between armies of France, Russia, England, and America. We, in our town, were under American occupation. But the war on the Front was over, the killing stopped there. We were now under curfew for months, no one could leave or enter our little town, of 350 people, after 6 p.m.

During the war I was in charge of the company's library. I was 20. Well, American soldiers took care of the library fast, and all of the books, regardless of their content, ended up in our Traun River, which was easy to reach by just opening the window and throwing them out. And so, we learned to adjust from the German occupation in 1938, to the American occupation, in 1945. The difference between the occupations was that with the Germans we could not express any opinions we had, but could come and go as we pleased; with the American occupation, we were restrained physically and had a curfew. All the hotels were occupied by Americans, and we had restricted access to places where only soldiers could go. We didn't like either one of them, but considered ourselves very lucky, as the horror stories from the Russian occupied portions of Austria reached us. Part of our family lived in those parts and later told us of the atrocities they had to endure. We had to get used to many changes because American soldiers were completely in charge of everything in our section.

There was an uneasy feeling among the population. The word was that America and Russia are getting ready to fight each other. That made the Hungarians in Austria very uneasy, as Hungary was under Russian control. I got a little ahead here, so let me step back and explain why that affected me personally.

Background note: Joska (my future husband) had been in the Cavalry, a Hungarian officer. When he was in Kiev, Russia, at an outpost in tents, he and his men were attacked by the Russian Army. All but three were killed. The three who survived laid in snow for 20 hours so as not to be seen. All were hospitalized, two were very damaged, Joska was released. Military men who had been released were given out to companies to work. Joska went to work for MOM.

In the last few months of the war, Budapest, the capital of Hungary, was surrounded by Russian troops for 90 days. Employees from the biggest company in Hungary, called MOM, (Magyar Optics, Hungarian Optics Works) that manufactured optical, laboratory, and surveying equipment for Zeiss in Germany, wanted to save the delicate equipment from falling into Russian hands. At a moment's notice, they had orders to bring it all to Austria. There was no time or telephones to notify their families. The clothes they were wearing was all they could take. These men left thinking they may never see their families and country again. Joska was one of them. None of them saw their parents alive again. Joska had to wait until the 1960's to be able to return as a US citizen. In addition to the men from this company, anyone who could flee from Russian occupied territory, made it to Austria as their first stop. On the train in route to Austria the bombs were falling as the Americans were bombing the train tracks…Joska and the other passengers jumped off the train and he lost the suitcase that had the few things he was able to pack.

Joska (Yo-sh-kah), officer on horseback

Joska in Russia WWII

Little did I know what impact all this would have on my future.

And why am I telling you all of this? Because here began the turn-around of my life. Now I have to tell you a little side-story:

> *I was 19 and in love with a cute Austrian boy. There was not a doubt in my mind that we are going to get married. A friend of mine had an aunt who read Tarot cards. When it was my turn, she said to me, looking me straight in the eye: 'You are not going to marry this guy....I see one coming from far away, and taking you even farther...I see a lot of water'. We laughed very hard, and I said, 'Sure, you have me mixed up with someone else. We are going to get married, and soon that will be'. As you can see, she was right after all. And almost made me a believer that those cards work. Our engagement fell apart a few months after. Now, back to the main story, which involves a guy from far away and a lot of water.*

Well, among the men who left with the company, was the man of my life who I spent the next 57 years with. That very handsome man, a truly genuine gentleman, stole my heart. His name was Joseph Vegvari, and just by looking at him you could feel a certain caring way, which was very captivating. In his struggling German language he told me about his service of almost two years on the Russian Front as an officer in the Hungarian Cavalry. After being wounded, he was spared going back to the Front, and was assigned to the company MOM. And that is what brought him to Theresienthal.

The next year, on a snowy winter day it was that we got married in my favorite Schloss Ort Kirche (Church), on February 23, 1946. That alone would probably fill many pages, which I may attempt to make a short story out of, but I can't promise it is going to be short.

Maybe a little explanation about the "Vegvari" name could not hurt, so here it is: Joska's name was Joseph Wagner when he was born to a Hungarian mother and a German father. His father came to Hungary as a young boy from Southern Germany in the early 1900. When Joska was a young man, the Hungarians with non-Hungarian last names were given the choice of choosing a Hungarian last name. So came the name Vegvari to life. It is a very beautiful name in that language…and a name that later created a lot of spelling problems, as my children well know.

1946

September 20, our family welcomes little Ilona Margit. If there ever was a baby loved and spoiled, that was her. (Ilonka means 'little' Ilona) Everything else was not important. She has taken my mother out of the depression she was in since my brother was killed in Russia. We were sharing an apartment with her because it was impossible to find one for us. The Hungarian-speaking son-in-law, struggling with the German language, created some funny situations. One of them was when my mother was standing quietly watching Joska bent over the bassinet, talking softly to his little daughter in Hungarian. I was in the kitchen when she came to me and whispered, "Do you know that Joska is talking Hungarian to the baby? Doesn't he know that she doesn't understand Hungarian?" I looked at her and I said, "I don't think she understands him, or me or you…she just enjoys a soft voice and a smiling face." I could see

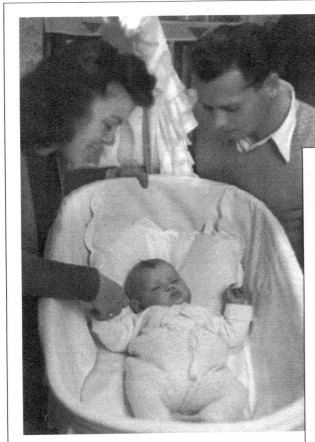

I traded my gold watch for the bassinet.

Oma with her baby

she heard me, but she was not convinced. Even with the language, there was never a harsh word spoken, my mother loved him very much.

By the year 1948, it became more and more obvious that our stay was a temporary arrangement, and some decision will have to be made. America was our first choice, but visas to America had a long waiting period of two to three years, and the Russians were too close.

Our private life was a happy but uneasy time, filled with uncertainty in regards to the Russian occupation in Hungary. We were thinking of going to Hungary, but that was no longer an option as we were hearing from people who have been lured back. Their train never stopped in Hungary, it took them straight to Siberia. As my husband had been an officer in the Hungarian Cavalry, we could not risk it, or even try it. Now other options had to be considered because of the uncertainty of a coming conflict hanging over Europe again. And people who lost their country were very much afraid that the Russians would get the upper hand and the men be sent to Siberia. So now we were looking around to find places to take into consideration. One option had to be considered, it was Argentina. The first look on the map told us this was a very long way from Austria. But it was an option we were told by the Consulate of Argentina, who thought if the whole group of approximately 20 specialists stays together, they could build an optical company. He got the visa for us and said he will help us organize the new company in Buenos Aires. "Sounds great!" was what all of us said. Knowing that the papers would soon be in our hands, the gypsy in me was wide awake and ready for whatever comes our way. And did it ever come.

Let me tell you a little mini story, which at this moment should be told:

I was 17, working in the textile office now, and I found myself doodling on the desk pad, pretending I am writing to myself, writing my name, and the address "Gretl Stockhammer, Amerika". I crossed it out so nobody would see it, because I really didn't know anything about America. We learned very little about the world outside Europe. Funny that I would end up in that neck of the woods and live out the last part of my life there. Who would have guessed? It only took us 10 years and a lot of water to cross, to find the right address.

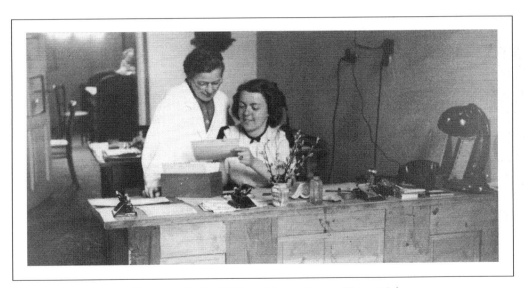

Theresienthaler Weberei (weaving-mill, textile)

My sister Resi worked as a Red Cross nurse during the war.

Joska in Russia, 1942

Joska, center, in his home town, Alsogod

Joska, far right, Russia, 1941-42

4

LEAVING AUSTRIA

SAYING GOODBYE TO MY HOMELAND

Our last days at home before leaving Austria
Trude, Resi, me, our mother. It was not deliberate,
and I don't know if anyone ever noticed,
but Max is included in the photo behind us.

Leaving Austria

SAYING GOODBYE TO MY HOMELAND

Christmas 1948

It was just a few days before we decorated the tree and were baking our last cookies for the most celebrated holiday of the year, and only Joska and I knew that in the next few weeks we had to leave. It was best not to share this with my mother and my sisters on this last Christmas together. There was always that little hope left for my mom that it would not happen, so why spoil the joyous days for all our so loving family. But as all things in life, the time came fast, and the date was set for January 17, 1949.

It was a cold winter morning and snow was falling as the whole family walked to the bus station by the Alt Mühl (Old Mill) Restaurant, our town's gathering place. Everybody's eyes looked like they did not have a lot of sleep, and had done a lot of crying overnight. While we waited, my mom handed me a bottle of baby formula for Ilonka. Resi, my oldest sister, took the warm socks off her feet, knelt down and put them on mine so I would be warm. Her husband, whom we called Gödi, (which means godfather, he was Ilonka's) could not let go of her. He was walking with her in his arms, tears running down his face. That is forever in my memory.

Mom put a lot of smoked ham and food that would not perish in one of the packages to take along. How could she have known that it would hold us over for one week in

Genoa? Ja, mothers always know things that the smart kids only find out when they are parents themselves. And now, with last hugs and promises to come back, we boarded the bus which was taking us to Linz, where we boarded a train to bring us to Genoa, Italy.

As the bus rolled away, the handkerchiefs they used could not wave well in the breeze, the tears made them too heavy to fly. I cried too, but my tears were always balanced out with expectation, curiosity, and excitement, for the things to come. We took the train to Linz to bring us over the Brenner Pass on the Italian/Austria border to Genoa. An American ship used during WWII to transport American soldiers back and forth was converted and now being used to transport the so-called 'displaced persons' of Europe to wherever they needed to be transported. We fit that description because Joska was displaced from his homeland. Our destination was Argentina.

When we arrived in Genoa, we were told that the ship had experienced a delay. Since it will take at least one week, we were to stay in what was called a 'lager' or, camp. This huge room, holding up to 500 bunk beds, was our home for the week. No heating was available. Remember, it was January, and Italy gets cold too, of course, not like Austria.

It was an uncomfortable week. The food was soup, for lunch and dinner, and everything you could think of, was in it. Joska made a decision, he said, "I eat the soup, and you and Ilonka substitute with all the things mom gave us when we left". Ja, that was him, as always, the caring and unselfish man.

After one week, the ship came and took on 1,100 passengers. The men on ship were separated from the women and children. Ilona and I had a cabin that we shared with a Hungarian lady from our group. The ship was very clean, and the crew was nice, although we did not understand one word, as none of us spoke English. The food was very good, but some things were strange. The maitre d' in the dining room was a tall, 6'5", good-looking, well-dressed, black man, who took a liking to Ilonka. He called her "my princess". He was the first black man she ever came in contact with. After he took her in his arms she wiped her hands to make sure the color did not come off. His laugh and smile from then on was a joy to see every day in the dining room.

After two weeks, we arrived in Buenos Aires. To unload 1,100 people into a so-called Immigration Hotel, took some time. But it was good to feel secure ground under our feet again.

...And here we are. What now?

A photographer came and took the last photos of our family. No one knew when the next time would be that we are together. Joska, Ilona, me, Josef (Pepperl, Trude's husband), Mom, Trude, Resi, Ferdinand (Gödi, Resi's husband).

Ilona with a traditional Hungarian dress, hand-sewn by Resi and me

Gmunden and the lake Traunsee

The mountains are, Grünberg, Traunstein, and the Schlafende Griechin. The Sleeping Grecian maiden who lays there turned to stone, according to legend. Our beautiful Schloss Ort is on a little island in the lake. The large building in front of the church steeple is the school where I went, and later where Ilona went to fourth grade.

5
START IN ARGENTINA

AND LIVING THERE

In the Plaza de Mayo park,
a favorite pastime

Joska and Ilona feeding the pigeons in front of the
Casa Rosada where Juan and Evita Peron lived.

Start in Argentina

AND LIVING THERE

February 1949

After 17 days on the ship, where men and women were separated, we arrived in Buenos Aires. 1,100 people poured into what was called an immigrant 'hotel'. The confusion was great. The language barrier now really became a problem. The rooms were so big, they held 200 bunk beds. At 6:00 am the wake-up call ARRIBA (my first word to learn) came loud and clear, and by 6:30 the room was empty and could not be used before bedtime. To describe the living for the next three weeks would fill a book by itself. So let me only focus on the most horrifying things.

Ilonka got the measles and had to be hospitalized in the 'Quarantine Room' with about 35-40 other children who either had the measles or the whooping cough. All these children were in one room, divided only by an eight foot curtain between these two contagious diseases. Every six hours they came and gave her a penicillin shot. It was the wonder drug for everything. I could stay with her, was given a chair, and told not to use the bed, day or night, where Ilonka was. Needless to say I broke the rule many times, and was warned every time I rested my legs or my head on her bed. Joska could only see me through the window from far away, as we were on the second floor.

After about five days, I laid myself across Ilonka on the bed and refused the shots they were giving her. Her little bottom began to look like a strawberry. They found a Russian doctor who spoke German to tell me they are going to send me back with Ilonka to the 'hotel' room, where about 50 children were held in that room. I told her that if they want them all there with the measles and the whooping cough, go ahead. I told them that the measles did not need penicillin, that it needed a darkened room. Not knowing the language does not mean you are automatically stupid! I saw the reaction on the doctor's faces as she translated it. The shots stopped. After two weeks in the hospital, we went back to join Joska in the 'hotel' again. By now we knew that the good consul was never to be found, and the optic company was in never-never land, or at least postponed to 'mañana' (tomorrow), the most famous word in the Argentine/Spanish language. Well, now began the hunt to find a place to live, and to work. Lots of people came to the 'hotel' looking for workers, maids, or whatever they needed. And so we pretended to have done this kind of work before, just to get out of there.

There were about 1000 people in what looked like a schoolyard, and there were eight benches. To get one of these to use during the day, Joska would get up at 5:00 in the morning and secure one so we had a place to sit. Otherwise, the grass was our place to sit until 6:00 p.m. when the rooms, or halls, were unlocked. Ilona was terrified to go to the bathrooms, as they were only just holes where you had to do what nature told you to do. So, Joska found a little potty we kept for her, otherwise she would fall back in her baby-age stage, there were no diapers. It was all these things together for us to take any work we could find just to get out of this hell. So that was why, when a nice couple came, looking for a maid, and was willing to take the three of us, we left in a minute.

Anything to get out of here was better. But was it? By this time our group had split like a broken cup in many pieces. There was no way to get that group together, as we were made to believe, to form an optic company. Everybody was on their own, nobody spoke the language, and we all looked at each other knowing we are on our own.

When we were shown the little shack in the backyard, sitting on a dirt floor with one small bed in there, we knew almost instantly what was waiting for us. By now it was the beginning of March. We were still wearing the winter clothes we left Europe with. But it was summer here, and all our belongings were in big crates stored by a Hungarian family, whose address was given to me by his sister in Gmunden, by coincidence. I think of them with so much love and thanks for the help they gave us, as we were complete strangers. He stored them for us in his cellar.

I was told what to do, as a maid. My day started at 6:00 in the morning with washing (by hand), cleaning, baking, and a lot of little things in between. My day ended at 10:00 p.m. Joska was looking for a job and found one through our new friend. It was a machine shop, something so strange to him. He had a degree in accounting and he had 30 people under him in the Estimating Division of a large company before the war. But we needed money, we had absolutely no money.

As the weeks went by, my nerves were stretched to the limit. The family had a little girl about Ilona's age. She had a huge box full of toys, and many times Ilona could not play with these toys. She was not allowed to. I prepared eggs for the little girl (something Ilona loved) and was not allowed to give one to Ilona. How do you explain to a two and a half year old she can't have an egg or banana? I could not buy it for the first few weeks until Joska got his first check. It came, and I bought bananas!!!

The third month we were invited to our new friends' home. I gave Joska a list to go there first and bring us fresh clothes from our crates, which were still stored in their cellar. He brought them, and got busy ironing the clothes. Three months in crates did not make them attractive, and he did a good job! He washed Ilona's hair and dressed her, as I had no time. After all this time I got my first half day off that Sunday, and we left to see Rosi and John.

Dressed as we were, the people now saw us in a different way. Our clothes were the latest European fashion because our apartment in Austria was company-owned and we paid no rent...and all my money went for clothes, and also my sister and I had sewn for weeks before we left. I can still to this day see their faces pressed on that front window as we left all dressed up to go to the train station. For the first time they saw us in a different way. And as we came home at 9:00 that evening they were sitting in the back yard with a Spanish/German dictionary in hand to ask questions.

They knew now that I never did this work for a living before, and we knew then that our days here now were numbered. Sure enough, on Wednesday we were given until Saturday to move. Move where? By now Joska had some money, not much, but he was looking with the help of our new friend to find the cheapest hotel in Buenos Aires, where we could stay for a few weeks. We are now used to sleeping all in one bed, and he found one with just that. At least, he said, we have a place to go to.

It was Friday now, and I got a call from Joska's workplace. A Hungarian man I did not know was trying to tell me something. But my knowledge of Hungarian was not good enough to understand him. All I could understand was the word 'hospital'. Joska was there, he cut off his finger below the first knuckle, and he was on his way home. Useless to say, the next few hours, not knowing anything, having to work and thinking of moving the next days, were probably the longest hours in my entire life. Now what will we do? There is no family to turn to for help. All our traveling European companions were on their own too and probably struggling along like we were. When, after 3:00 p.m. Joska came, his face was white as a sheet, in so much pain, and all he said was, "I lost my finger, what am I going to do?" The pain was unbearable, and all he was given was aspirin. But my work had to be done, our suitcases had to be packed, and the woman demanded I bake a cake before we leave because she was having company. Ilonka was holding Joska's hand and kept hugging him. She was a child who adjusted to everything. That was a gift to us.

We left the next morning and found our hotel. No bathroom, a toilet down the hallway. We stayed there for four weeks until our friend found us a house, one room, a kitchen, and a bathroom. By then it was mid May and I can say "hell" was over. Nothing could get worse than the last four months. We have been through an endurance test, and survived together. We now could get our seven crates out and unpack the many things we had stored in our friend's cellar. Among them were a few hundred cigarette lighters. When we left Austria, Joska's company could not pay their workers the final wages, so they paid them with cigarette lighters. These we smuggled in by making a false bottom in our crates. Our friend sold them for us and that gave us the start to buy furniture.

Joska's middle finger was getting better, he lost only about one and a half inches.

He thought he had lost the whole finger. Now he could work again and we started to make our first home. To this day, it was the best. We made a home out of crates and imagination, and it worked. I was never prouder in my life than in our first home. The first thing I did was empty out a crate, put a table cloth on it, unpack a vase, and put flowers on the table. Now it was home. It did not matter that for half a year my cooking had to be done on a one-flame propane burner like campers, that we had no shower, that I had on many days to hide and tell Ilonka, when the milk or water delivery came, that we are playing a game: just don't make a sound. Because there was not one dime in the house.

In a country where meat was the staple, and cheap, we could not afford it. It did not matter. We were trained in the years before we came here. Meat was just not available then, but for different reasons. In wartime in Austria four ounces of meat per week is what we used to live on. One gets creative with the choices. 'Where' do I put this week's four ounce ration in? On a sandwich? Or in an extended gravy where you have to play hide and seek with the meat?

All these months I could not write to my mother because the truth I could not say, and lying was not an option for me. I could not find the words to make up a life when ours was so terrible. When we had the first home is when I first wrote.

As the months went by, guess what? The consul from Vienna woke up to the fact that he now wants to create a company with the remaining people. Well it was a little late, as half of them went who-knows-where. About eight or nine stayed and said they will give it a try. What it meant was we had to move about 800 km northwest of Buenos

Aires, to a small place, I mean small, a little town called Rojas. There we found a house to rent and a somewhat normal life began to take shape. The men had work, and we learned to adjust to a slow paced life. Just being a housewife and mother was a normal life and I was content with it. There were four Austrian girls in this group from my home town in Gmunden, and we formed a very close friendship and had some good times together. Ilona's blonde hair, the only one in this whole town, made her special, and got us free photographs from a photographer.

When I got my first letter from my mother, it had about 30 pages dated almost daily. She had no address to send them to. She wrote them, saved them in the months when I put her through the most trying time of her life. I knew it, but the truth would have killed her. My sister wrote: If you do that one more time, you can come home and bury your mother. As I found out, she lost 30 pounds in the months of my silence. I was not surprised. To this day I cannot say if I did wrong in not writing. I have often asked that question myself without finding the answer. Lying was not an option and my whole being was against telling her the truth.

After four years in Argentina, the company Joska worked for closed, and we again had to pack up. The little town we spent the last three years, had nothing to offer. By this time, an old friend (Kalman and Hilde Avar) who ended up in the Dominican Republic was writing and asking us to consider to come. It could not come at a better time. Well, packing up was what we became expert in, and that is just what we did. As I said, the gypsy was awake and well! So we left with our friends Christl and Imre Szilas and their little boy Werner. We left the little town of Rojas, went to Buenos Aires, and from there to a different world.

Note: When I started writing, I did not think that Argentina would take so much room in my storybook. It has captivated me as I started writing, depressed me when the hard times there became a life, and puzzled me how I could live through all of it and never ask myself: Why on earth did I leave my secure home, a good job, and all my family in Austria?

The question never came up. It just never did.

6

LEAVING ARGENTINA–
TO THE DOMINICAN REPUBLIC

Going through the Panama Canal
on our way to the Dominican Republic.
Imre Szilas, me, Christl Szilas,
their son Werner, and Ilona.

Leaving Argentina–
to the Dominican Republic

As I look around me and I am seeing my friends in this train station, their eyes and mine are looking as eyes do, just before they let go of their tears. I am putting on a brave face to cover the heartache that is coming on stronger with every passing minute. The train whistle tells me to start to say goodbye now. We knew that it was again a final goodbye to our friends who became family in these past years. Mixed with fears and expectations of the unknown, we are about to start a new chapter in our life. We waived our handkerchiefs from the train window. And as the train left, that was the final view I remember.

A long trip across the Argentine pampas had begun, endless it seems, for hours and hours. Our excitement was great as it ended and we saw mountains coming up. We had left the flat lands and slowly the train reached 7,000 meters at the Chilean border. For the first time that she could remember, Ilonka saw the snow. The train stopped, and she and Werner went outside and threw snowballs at each other. After a few hours downhill, we were in Valparaiso. Here we had to wait for the ship that would take us along the the South American West Coast, guide us through the Panama Canal and take us to Curaçao.

We were now seeing the end of our ship's cruise, as Curaçao was just one day away. A very hot and humid day in that port was waiting for us, it was December and that meant summer. We now made the last arrangements for our trip to Santo Domingo. We boarded a small plane and a few hours later we were greeted by our friends who had arranged a job for Joska. This time, we had a house to move into. It was empty, and we started all over again.

What a different world it was! Gone were the pampas, there were lush palm trees and greens wherever your eyes wandered. One thing was for certain, we did not have to worry about winter clothes.

We lived in a small European community with about 40-50 houses built around the *Armeria* (armory) where all the men worked. You could find families from Germany, Hungary, and Austria, creating a little 'hometown' atmosphere in a very strange surrounding. A two block walk away from it and that was the real island folks, which was 99% black and poor. But for once, we did not have a new language to learn.

It was a different life style. We all had maids, they came mornings and left early afternoon. The vendors, women with huge wooden trays on top of their head, came down the streets every day with fresh vegetables and fruits calling out their goods. No one had a car, taxies were not expensive. On Sundays many of us went to our favorite beach, Palenque, where the kids learned to swim in the waist-deep clear warm ocean. They loved it. We saw the native boys climbing up the enormously tall coconut trees, barefooted, to get us the green coconuts to drink. There was no refrigerator to have, so Joska solved the problem and built one. We got a block of ice and it was holding the food for one day until the iceman came the next day with a new block. This was the man my sister Resi warned me about: 'How can you leave here with a man who can't even hammer in a nail'. Not only did he build the refrigerator, but he built our bookcases, an outside bowling game, and a beautiful rocking horse later for our Timi. I was very proud of him. Ilonka and Christl Hund, our German friend's daughter, went to the Catholic School and were picked up by a horse-drawn carriage to go to and from school. Walking was too hot and the way was too long. As I said, this part of the world never gets cool.

After a few months being there and having taken a good look at our budget, we were somewhat concerned that we were unable to save money. It took all the money Joska got to break even, and women working did not exist. Well, how in the world are we going to have the $1,000 security the American Consul said we had to show before they issue a visa?

So, I was thinking, if I cook for four or five single engineers, who came from Austria to install a big project in the Armeria, how would that help? I have a maid to clean up, and by now my cooking experience is a lot better that in my Argen-

tine camp adventure! Hey, it worked!! The guys were so happy, and five days a week I cooked for them. The money was set aside until we knew that that will not stop us to get where we eventually will go.

Our lives settled in very nicely among our old and new friends and we knew this is the place to think about expanding our family and giving Ilona a sister or brother. Well, it worked, and I got pregnant.

There were three women pregnant among the Europeans, all hoping to get a boy, because they all had girls. The first two were ahead of me to give birth, I was the last one to give birth. Bets were going on among the guys.

On Sunday evening about 9:00 p.m., my water broke. Now we could not find a taxi at this hour, so a German friend who had a car offered us a ride from San Cristobal (where we lived) to the city, Ciudad Trujillo, where the hospital was…about 60 km away. So on the road we go. My pain was here, but bearable, and they were not so close, that meant we would make it. AHA! But life is giving us another little adventure. A flat tire in the middle of nowhere, in the darkness, was not really the excitement we needed. My thoughts were: two men and me, and neither of them knows what to do. No phone and no houses in sight. The only lights were the headlights. Well…let's just say I talked to that baby of mine. "Slow down, it is not the time to be anxious to see the mess we are in." He listened.

Finally we got the tire exchanged and after another half hour we saw the lights of the city. In the excitement, our friend took a few wrong turns as he had no idea where the clinic was, and I lost complete orientation (one of my talents that Joska has always accused me of). Well, it was dark, and I must say my driver was cursing all the way to the clinic. He finally located it, it was 11:30 p.m. I sent them all home, after all, Ilona was there to be taken care of.

For the next 10 hours I was walking and hurting, and the baby took my previous advice to slow down too seriously. (I think that was the first and last time he listened to me.) After 12 hours of labor, we got our son. I told the doctor, when my husband comes, please don't tell him it is a boy. But by the face of Joska when he walked in my room, I knew, the doctor did not keep his promise. Well, he could not wait to go back and tell his buddies that he had a son, and he won the bet. It was December 20th, and I told the doctor that I will not stay here on Christmas. So he let me go. And on Christmas Eve, December 24th, 1953, we put him under the tree, where he gave us his first proof that his voice can be strong and demanding, that little voice, it never changed. Our son was three weeks old before we could agree on a name. He was christened Tivadar Mathias Vegvari in the beautiful church in San Cristobal.

Timi was a free little spirit who loved to play and climb outside with the native little boys. None of them were ever wearing shoes, so he forever took his off, and we forever were looking for them. He, thank God, did not follow the boys fashion of just wearing a shirt that was too small and came only to their navel, and nothing else. Why a shirt? That is what I never understood.

These were good times, but as we could see, this was not, after all, our final destination. Slowly, as the years went by, the Europeans began to exit to either back home, or to the USA. We applied for a visa and a *salida* (exit papers). That was risky all by itself.

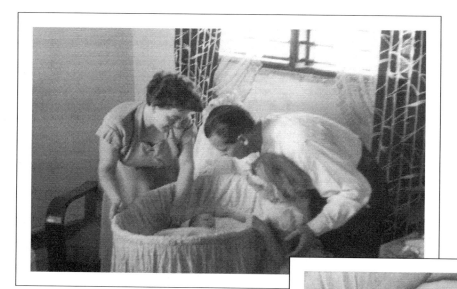

Tivadar Mathias is home.

Joska worked for an armory that was run by a Hungarian, Mr. Kovaz. Mr. Kovaz was very powerful and well connected to Presidente Trujillo. If he found out in any way that his employees wanted to leave the country, he could stop it. It all had to be done in secret by everyone. We applied, and we knew it would take years before this is going to happen, as the quota system in the US was strictly enforced. We were in no hurry, the company Joska worked for was doing okay so far.

The heat was doing Ilona no good, she was a very thin little girl. The heat was getting to her. Her appetite was not anywhere it should be. When I sent some of her and Timi's pictures to my family in Austria, they said: 'Send her to us, this little girl needs the mountain air, we fatten her up.' I was jokingly mentioning this one day. Her eyes lighted up and she said, 'Oh, can I go to see Oma, mami? Can I?' Well, kids say a lot of things in a moment and don't think about it, so we kind of laughed it off. But she kept asking, and we knew she was serious. I could see that she was like me in that way, and so it came to it that in October 1955, we put her on PanAm to leave us for a while. There were no jets, this was four propellers, it took two days to get there, and they were the longest days, until we got a telegram: '*Sie ist in den Armen der Familie*'....She is in the arms of the family. Needless to say, we finally got some good night's sleep, and my crying slowed down.

Thinking back, these were times where people could be trusted, and the fears we are experiencing today came not even in our thoughts. I guess the world was a totally different one then, children were more protected, as they should be. Now, the only communication we had were letters, and it took weeks for a letter to go one way. The letters from her were all in Spanish, but as time went by, the German words mixed in,

Mom putting on a brave face, while Ilona left with a smile

From this thin, pale little girl, Ilona changed quickly to a healthy rosy-cheeked child.

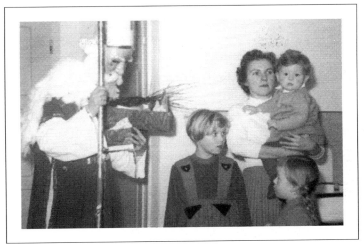

Trude with Sissi and Susi, and our girl. What a difference in just three months!

Ilona on a 4th grade school outing on the Grünberg (Green Mountain)

and soon, all in German, and these were a treasure to read.

It is now March 1957, it was time to get our family together again. I took Timi, now three years old, and we were on our way to get our little girl home. We boarded a German freighter in Ciudad Trujillo that was taking us to Italy, and from there by train home to Austria.

When I stepped out of the train in Gmunden and saw Ilonka, I knew we did the right thing, the red-cheeked healthy looking mountain girl with little braids I could hold in my arms told me so. All the tears I shed in the last one and a half years were worth it for the life she could experience. I know she will always cherish it, and she does, with all her heart, still today.

After six months in Austria with my mother, who I had not seen since we left in 1949, we embarked on a ship and went back to Santo Domingo to my husband, who had been alone and very anxious to get us all back. We moved from San Cristobal to the capital, Ciudad Trujillo. Now, waiting for the US Consul to notify us about the progress on our application for the visa became nerve wracking. After all, we started applying in 1953, some people waited even longer than we. We were lucky that we could use the Austrian quota, which was better, since not many Austrians were eager to leave their country. So, the end of December 1958, we packed up again. This time only with suitcases, no crates with mattresses and rugs…everything had to be left there. Even our house that we bought was left without us being compensated for it.

We said goodbye to friends, again. Some of them we knew would end up somewhere in the US, depending when they got their visa. But this is a big country, and who knows where they find their place and a permanent home. By now it seems we are experts in saying goodbye to friends we treasure, and tears come easily when you know this is again another goodbye.

Note: I don't know, again the memories take over and the pages are getting more and more far from what I intended to write. And still, I think I only scratched the surface.

Christmas 1954, San Cristobal

Timi on the horse that his daddy made for him

We have two beautiful children.

A birthday party and a first crush, Carmen!

Our home

7

TO THE USA

THE FINAL DESTINATION

The American Family
one Hungarian, two Austrians, one Dominican

TO THE USA

THE FINAL DESTINATION

1958

The day finally came, after numerous secret trips to the American Consulate, that we were told we passed all the required tests and now we can pick up the so long awaited visas. The salida was approved, and Joska finally could give notice to the company.

The last few weeks we were living in a hotel in the capital. This hotel was a place where many Europeans transitioned, they had just arrived and were waiting for a place to stay, or they had given up their homes and were waiting to leave. We had given away some, and sold some of our furniture and belongings. This time we could not take it with us in crates like before. We now are only carrying our suitcases on our new adventure, a new start, indeed, again.

This goodbye was a lot easier, as we knew many of our friends will follow us sooner or later to find their permanent home in the USA. On December 29, 1958 we boarded the plane for Miami. By now we had kind of mastered the Spanish language in the last 10 years, but here now comes another one to learn. Poor Joska, languages were just not his greatest talent. From Hungarian to German, to Spanish, and now English at the age of 42.

We stayed in Miami one day and then boarded the train that will take us across the US to the West Coast, end station Los Angeles, California. And so began the last part of our journey, knowing when we get off this train, we are there.

Ilona brought her accordion to the train compartment we shared with two American women. When they asked her to play, she did just that. At least we thought that is what they asked, as we did not speak or understand the language. After all, it was New Year's Eve, let's sing. When we stopped for a while in Kansas, it was snowing. For Timi, our five year-old, seeing his first snow was quite an experience. All he could say was a shocked "But this is COLD!!"

After almost two days, we reached the state of California. My eyes were looking for the flowers I have read about, and all I saw was flat land, no trees, and little green. Is this another Argentine pampa? Are there mountains? I have read books about the blooming California desert, where is it? Well, it was January, and the desert blooms in April, as I found out later. What I did not realize was that Los Angeles was called, I once read, a city in the desert. My only knowledge of California came from a book I love very much, *Kalifornische Symphony*, in English, *The Hallelujah Trail*.

We arrived in L.A., and friends we learned to love in Santo Domingo were there as we came off the train. These friends were now our sponsors, they signed papers for us to be responsible should we get in financial troubles, they made it possible to come here. They rented a furnished apartment in Glendale for us near them. What a different start that was, compared to the previous ones we lived through. Food was in the refrigerator, it was an overwhelming experience for us. It was January 2, 1959. The next day was my birthday, and Joska went shopping for roses with Titus Radisay, our friend's son. It was the first purchase in our new homeland. What a start!

January 1959

We are starting over, again. Once more, but for the last time, everything around us has changed. We learned really fast that one of the necessities here is a car. Joska needed to take lessons from a friend to pass the DMV test, which he quickly did. Our first car, purchased for $800, was a big investment and would have taken all the money we had left. So, we learned a new word, 'credit'. $400 got us the car, and a chance to establish a credit. I did not understand how this will do it, but 35 years later, buying another car, the salesman came back after checking our credit and said, 'Since 1959 you were never late on any payment…in 37 years'. It was 1996, 'Take any car, give me one dollar until you sign the deal'. I guess it was a good start then.

In Glendale, where we ended up staying, another new word came to light, it was 'smog'. What is smog? Joska's breathing problems, which he had never had, were so severe, it was frightening. One weekend we were visiting our friends, Hilde and Kalman Avar, who had come a year earlier. They lived in Gardena. The fog rolled in and we could not go back to Glendale. Joska and I were very worried because he did not have his asthma medication with him, but he had no breathing problem whatsoever for those two days. One hour back in Glendale, Joska started wheezing again. Well, that did it! We moved fast from there, and ended up for the next 12 years in Gardena. Ilona started school there, she was 12-1/2 and learning English. For her it was not a big thing, as by now she handled Spanish, German, and some Hungarian, extremely well. Timi was five years old and was not that eager to go to school. Not only was it his first time in school, but he did not speak the language. His first day was a true adventure, and if you want to know more about it, check the "Short Stories" section in the back.

Time passed, Joska was working, and so was I. Our dream to save to buy a home, if we don't splurge on anything, took on reality, and the day came when we found the dream house.

2509 W. 144 Street, Gardena, CA   Phone: DAvis 38145

Joska built us a beautiful patio with a waterwheel. Once again he proved my sister wrong! Then came a not so little side-splurge on a Shetland pony for Timi. This was an investment he will treasure for the rest of his life. He filled his room with barrel-racing trophies, and we always knew where we would spend our Sunday afternoons, and where he would spend every minute of his free time. It was with Vega, his pony.

Timi and Vega, the trophy-winning team

This was the perfect reason for Joska to quit smoking. He reasoned that it would offset the stable fee, and my new carpet that I planned, would wait another year, with a convincing statement: 'When Timi grows up, he won't remember our new carpet, but he will remember having a pony.'

Joska's job, thank God, has moved him away from the machine shop and he was now working for Cinerama Co. on very hi-tech film industry cameras. He had the patience for this kind of work, and he was good. He never got back to his original trade for which he had a degree, finance. He was a very knowledgeable person, who you could ask any historical, geographic, or mathematic question, and he had the answer. But he could not overcome the language barriers. Joska could read the newspaper or journals and understand fully, it was communicating that was difficult. He played endless, difficult puzzles and word games in both German and Hungarian, but not English.

Many of our friends from the old country were in similar situations, and we all learned to cope. In spite of my limited knowledge in English, I found also a good job. Will you believe me if I say it was in Sales/Customer Service, talking six to eight hours on the phone with people from all over the US and the world? When I was offered the job I asked my future boss, "Do you know what you are doing?" He said, "Good or bad English, you always get the point across, and I am not worried!"

And so it was, 23 years and 23 bosses (many who I had to train), that finally I got the title 'Distributor Sales Manager'. Remember, this was 1985, and women still had to fight their way up every step of the way. And you better believe I did this without hanky-panky.

I retired in 1986 at the age of 63. Joska was already in pension since 1978. In 1979, my dear mother left this world and I am so grateful that I visited her in Austria ever so often, so did our children, and granddaughter, Micheli. My mother was in the loving care of my two sisters, Resi and Trude. Unfortunately, our mother had to say goodbye to Resi, her oldest child, who died before her in 1974 at the age of 59.

Life took on a normal every-day pace. My sister Trude and husband Josef (Pepperl) visited us and we proudly showed them our new homeland. Joska and I traveled a lot, revisited the places we once called home, and explored as much as time and money allowed us to see in our new one. Every year we made one big trip, building an inventory in our memory bank, to share later when traveling would be no longer comfortable. Hoping to have these memories, which is really all we have left when age is hindering us to keep gathering them.

So we built these memories one by one, together, and hoped they stay with us.

8
OUR LAST SUNSET

2003

Our Last Sunset

2003

I'd like to skip the years now because my two children have their own memories in their now-permanent homeland.

For many years, I am now retired, like Joska. It is the year 2000, and once again a new unknown word is beginning to emerge, one that is frightening and unthinkable that it could happen to us. Nothing prepared us for this.

We all know, older people are getting forgetful, that is how it is. So, it really takes time to face the fact and to find out where the normal memory-loss ends and something else emerges. Maybe one does not want to open the door to the reality, afraid what you might find behind it. It must have been that way. Slowly, strange days mixed with good ones made it clear, something is happening to my Joska, my gentle, dear, Dody…so strange that it was time to start opening that door.

What was behind that door became the truth, and now we knew he had to live with his tormented mind, which for him was 'reality'. I could see this in his frustrated, worried face. I am so sorry that it took me so long to understand, to handle it right. Explanations never worked. I learned that, maybe not fast enough. Nights were the worst, he did not find peace, and neither did I. All the talking did not help, Sundowner

Syndrome, Alzheimer, they named it.

There was Christmas 2002 coming, and his grandchildren and great grandchildren coming here. It was a good day for all, and especially for him. I watched him with Macy, she was combing his hair, they were having the time of their lives together. Nathan and Macy were competing to sit on his lap talking to him. I am sure he did not understand what they were saying. I don't think they even noticed. Until this day, this has formed a special bond they will never forget.

In my memory, I try to wipe out all the things that tarnish the gentle, loving, man he always was, in good and bad times. My most treasured is the day before the tragedy happened. It was the last one, and that day he was mine, all mine. We went to Redondo Beach, taking in the view of the waves, as we did so often, picking up dinner and going home. After dinner, as it was every evening, we were playing Rummicube, putting on *Heino* songs, Austrian music. He always wanted me to sing along, it was as if he could not play without it. He won two games. The whole day together was so pleasant and normal, he was so peaceful and content. When he went to bed I thought that was the best day we had in a long, long, time. Later when I went to bed, he was asleep, and I was happy I could get a good nights sleep also, after many sleepless nights. I thanked God for that wonderful day. He was the only one who knew it was to be the last day in our home.

The tragic events after that day were shared by both of my children, who stood by their father and me. So, I will not write about it. The children lived with me through it all, and can tell their children.

Opa has a place in all our hearts, and yours, Opa, is in our home.

Our last Christmas together
(back row) Nathan, Max, Macy, Samantha,
our great grandchildren and
(front) Adam and Michele, our grandchildren

Macy and Opa

Short Stories

Short Stories

- Austria 87
- Hungary 111
- Argentina 119
- Santo Domingo (Dominican Republic) 133
- USA 141

A Question You Are Probably Asking

Why are there so many short stories?

It is all Ilona's fault! Over the years she heard a great many of these 'happenings', and so as I concentrated on the Life-Changing events, she kept asking and kind of demanding, "You have to put in this…and this…it can't be left out!" Timi was right there with her with the demands! Well, that would mean I write a book, which was the farthest thing in my plans. What I settled for was the Short Stories, or episodes, whatever you like to call them, independent from the big events, but from the different stages of my life that would give some background.

The problem was, too many came to mind, overwhelming me. So, here they are, one by one. This way we both had our way: it is not a book, and the stories are a 'side-order'!

Austria

Das Streichholz Mäderl

THE LITTLE MATCHBOX GIRL
AUSTRIA, 1927
Short Story

It was fall 1927, and about seven or eight months after I lost my father. Most of my days I was lucky enough to spend at our *Kinderheim* (children's home), run by a group of loving and caring Catholic nuns. Mom was working in the textile company (Theresienthaler Spinnerei und Weberei) and she, at least, had not to worry about the children. If you needed full day for the little ones, or after-school was needed, the Kinderheim was there.

As it was an old custom, during Advent and Christmas time, the children performed a play which involved small children, teenagers, and, if needed, grown-ups. It always was a packed house and it was quite famous because of the quality the sisters insisted or demanded from all of the performers. This year's play stayed with me, it was just too close to reality.

This years play was a three-act performance and was called *The Little Matchbox Girl*. The lead role was a little girl who lost her father. The sisters found the little girl who could fill that spot perfectly. Yes, I don't need to tell you, it was me. One problem was that I was not even five years old, and had to memorize all the lines, as I could not read. The sisters must have been very patient with me, because it worked.

In the last scene in Act III, the little girl is standing at the grave-site of her father. In the grave next to her father's was buried a little girl, and her parents were standing there, mourning her. I don't think, and I was told later, there was not a dry eye in the theater, as everyone knew about my loss. I did not have to pretend to cry, it came easily. The sisters even had their handkerchiefs ready during rehearsals. I don't know how my mother, sitting in the theater, could watch all that. But she knew I loved to be in that play, and that is how it was always for my mother, her children came first. Note: In the German version, *The Little Matchbox Girl* goes home with the mourning parents and has a home and a family.

Kinderheim in Theresienthal

This is where we children went during the day or after school.
The nuns and a priest lived there, mass was held in the chapel.
Later, Ilona had her first communion there.

The Rolling Bread or Mannah from Heaven

AUSTRIA, 1930
Short Story

It was my turn to go and buy the bread this evening from the bakery, which was about a five-minute walk on a dirt road from us. The road was just a path, and not kept up, so when it rained you had better watch where you put your feet.

"Hold on to the money," mom said, "this is the last schilling I have right now until I get paid."

I was buying a big double size round bread it was about the size of a large pizza, but about four to five inches thick. As I was on my way home, holding that bread in front of me, I did not see a puddle filled with rainwater. The bread and I ended up in it. All I could think was 'that was the last schilling', and now there are two more days of school this week, and we needed it for lunch. I made a U-turn back to the bakery. The bakerwife who knew me well, took one look and saw a crying dirty little girl, with a loaf of soggy dirty, bread in her hand.

All I said to her was, "That was the last schilling my mom has, I can't go home without bread." She cleaned me up a little, wiped my tears, and gave me a fresh loaf. It was a gift I have never forgotten. Every time afterwards when I went there, a special bond stayed with me and the baker…and it only was a loaf of bread. But at this time it was the biggest gift ever given to me.

    When I came home my mom took a look at me said, "What happened to you? Your dress is all dirty.   Good thing you fell before you had the bread."

Much later I told her the story, and she thanked the baker for it.

Revisiting the house where we lived, and where my father died in 1927. It is the house to the right of the sign.

Mutti's Rent Money

AUSTRIA, 1931
Short Story

(clockwise from left) me, Resi, Max, Trude , and our mother

We lived in the upstairs apartment of a house. The landlord and his wife lived downstairs. After my dad died, our mother worked in the textile factory about one mile below us in Theresienthal, along the river Traun. In a 48 hour week, she brought home about 15 Schillings.

One day my mother decided to clean out all the drawers in our credenza. The next thing I see is my mother frantically going through every drawer, and then her panic-stricken face as she opened the door to the wood-burning stove looking for the things she threw in to burn.

I remember her sitting in front of it on a little footstool, tears running down her face, repeating, over and over:

"I think I burned the rent money."

"I have to pay it this weekend." She said, "I put it in an envelope, and thinking it was empty, I must have put it in to burn with the other papers....and now we will be evicted because I don't have it." My mother would not stop crying.

Our landlord was tight with money, and greedy. He even counted the apricots on his tree where the branches reached our upstairs window to make sure we would not eat any. Without saying anything to her, I went downstairs. Only the landlady was home. I said to her:

"My mom is crying so much because you will throw us out of the house because she burned the rent money and we don't have any more money."

She looked at me and she said, "Don't say anything to Mr. Hausherr (Mr. Landlord), I have a little money on the side....if your mother can pay me back five Schillings a month for the next three months...go and tell her not to say anything."

I flew up the stairs with wings telling her the good news. She just looked at me like I was a good fairy. Her eyes red from crying, lightened up. She just shook her head and slowly her face, with all the love and goodness, came to life, even a smile found a place again. I must have been the happiest seven year-old there, because I felt I had saved our home.

14 Days, only 14 Days

GMUNDEN, AUSTRIA, 1943
Short Story

Yes, it was wartime, and everything around us would not let us forget it. But is there anything that stops young people from dreaming and planning the future?

As always for the last few months, we, Lotte, Steffi, Emma, and I, had our monthly get-together. This time we had a special reason, as Emma was leaving the next day to meet her husband of about one year. She was joining him in Germany to stay there with him. He was an officer stationed there.

"Let's all of us tell our plans we have for the future, OK? Come on! Emma is leaving tomorrow to be with her husband and all we can do is wish that her dream will come true".

"Steffi, what do you think you will do when Rudi is back?"

"Oh, as soon as he comes home, we'll get married. I want at least three children, so does he."

Lotte was the most intelligent one in our group. She had her PhD and could write beautiful poetry. She looked at us and said:

"I probably will get married, but first I'd like to explore a little the world outside this small town. Teaching is very much on my mind, so, my fiancé and I agreed that is the road we would like to take together."

My turn came. I said almost the same thing, only my plan to get married was much closer to be a reality. Just a couple of months away. As we ended our evening in this lovely home, we said goodbye to Emma, as she would leave early the next morning.

What are two weeks in a lifetime, one would ask. As we learned, your whole life and all your plans and dreams can change.

1. First it was Emma who came back from Germany. Her heart was broken. When she arrived, she found her husband living with another woman, stating he will marry her and divorce Emma. So, Emma, being in a strange country, she did the only thing she could, she came back home. She never got over that and never remarried.

2. Next was Steffi. Her fiancé lost his life that week on the Russian Front. So there went her dream. A dream, that was all she was left with. She also never got over him, and never married.

3. Lotte got bad news the very next day. She lost the man she wanted to share her life with. He lost his life in France, fighting there. She stayed single for the rest of her life.

4. So, I was the only one with all my plans in tact. Lucky me! But not for longer than a week that would be. I received a letter from my fiancé that he has found somebody else, and that he would marry her.

It can't be! I was reading the letter over and over again in disbelief. My seamstress was ready to start the wedding dress. It just can't be. But it was.

My whole world collapsed with that one page letter.

Was it just two weeks ago that four young women dreamed and planned? What can 14 days do in ones life. Just 14 days is all that it took.

But I was still the lucky one. Remember the man from far away that would take me with him over a lot of water? Three years later he did, and kept me for 57 years.

...My dream came true after all.

Wie Einst Lili Marleen

THE SONG OF THAT TIME
AUSTRIA, 1945
Short Story

In the last few months of the war, we saw that American bombers were flying over Austria reaching farther north, searching for German strongholds to drop their bombs. Vienna was in their path to reach the intended locations. That triggered many parents to send their children to small towns in the western and southern part of Austria, as some bombs fell in Vienna.

So, when the war ended, and Austria was divided among four occupiers (Russia, America, England, France), the children could not go back to Vienna for quite some time. Nobody was allowed to cross the Russian occupied eastern part, in which Vienna was. To make things worse, mail service was not working across this zone very good either.

My friend Emma, who came from Vienna a couple of years earlier to work in Gmunden, did find out that her nephew from Vienna was one of these children. He was about 25 miles from Gmunden, staying with a family in a small mountain village called Bad Aussee. The parents had not heard from him in the last few months and were very concerned. They were begging Emma to find him and let them know, if possible, how their boy was coping with this. So, when she was asking me to go with her, I could not refuse. It was Sunday. We had no problem getting there by train. Little Max, as we found out was in very good hands. That was all we wanted to know. We stayed with him until it was time to go.

It was late afternoon, and we found out there were no more train connections to go back to Gmunden. No rooms for overnight staying were available. What are we going to do? "Go on the road", was suggested, "maybe a car will give you a lift." So, we started walking the only street out of this village, up a steep mountain pass, the Potschen Pass, hoping a car could give us a lift at least to the next village. But, who in this year, 1945, had a car? No Austrian had a private car then.

We must have walked and stood there for a few hours, when Emma said to me, "All we see are American jeeps with soldiers, you see that? Why don't you try to wave to let them know you need a ride? You are the younger and prettier one, they will stop for you. But don't leave me!"

A jeep really stopped and we got into the car. Emma got a seat in front, and the two soldiers in the back squeezed me in. I almost sat on their laps. There was talking, but nobody understood what was said, until one of them said, "Sing Lili Marleen!" That song was so famous, even to the American soldiers. It probably was the most famous song at this time. Every night at 10:00 pm, it was ending the radio programs. It was a catching song and they wanted to learn it.

Well, let me tell you, by the time we reached Gmunden, these fellows had learned their first German song. And it occupied them so completely, they didn't have time to think of other things that we were worried about! When we arrived at my friend's house that she was sharing with relatives, we showed them the wrong house. These fellows were not very pleased that they could not come in. That is not what they hoped for. We made a promise that the next Sunday we would meet them for a boat ride on the lake. That did the trick, and they left. Was I glad! No, we did not honor that promise. Come Sunday, we saw them, from behind the window, trying to find us, driving up and down the street. Sorry, fellows!

I cannot hear that Lili Marleen song without thinking of that 25 mile teaching trip.

Lili Marleen

Vor der Kaserne
Vor dem großen Tor
Stand eine Laterne
Und steht sie noch davor
So woll'n wir uns da wieder seh'n
Bei der Laterne wollen wir steh'n
Wie einst Lili Marleen.

Unsere beide Schatten
Sah'n wie einer aus
Daß wir so lieb uns hatten
Das sah man gleich daraus
Und alle Leute soll'n es seh'n
Wenn wir bei der Laterne steh'n
Wie einst Lili Marleen.

Schon rief der Posten,
Sie blasen Zapfenstreich
Das kann drei Tage kosten
Kam'rad, ich komm sogleich
Da sagten wir auf Wiedersehen

Lilli Marlene

Underneath the lantern,
By the barrack gate
Darling I remember
The way you used to wait
T'was there that you whispered tenderly,
That you loved me,
You'd always be,
As once, Lilli Marlene

Time would come for roll call,
Time for us to part,
Darling I'd caress you
And press you to my heart,
And there 'neath that far-off lantern light,
I'd hold you tight ,
We'd kiss good night,
As once, Lilli Marlene

Orders came for sailing,
Somewhere over there
All confined to barracks
was more than I could bear

Wie gerne wollt ich mit dir geh'n
Mit dir Lili Marleen.

Deine Schritte kennt sie,
Deinen zieren Gang
Alle Abend brennt sie,
Doch mich vergaß sie lang
Und sollte mir ein Leids gescheh'n
Wer wird bei der Laterne stehen
Mit dir Lili Marleen

Aus dem stillen Raume,
Aus der Erde Grund
Hebt mich wie im Traume
Dein verliebter Mund
Wenn sich die späten Nebel drehn
Werd' ich bei der Laterne steh'n
Wie einst Lili Marleen

I knew you were waiting in the street
I heard your feet,
But could not meet,
With you Lilli Marlene

Resting in our billets,
Just behind the lines
Even tho' we're parted,
Your lips are close to mine
You wait where that lantern softly gleams,
Your sweet face seems
To haunt my dreams
As once, Lilli Marlene

The English translation has very little to do with the German lyrics.
It sounds like it was mostly an attempt to rhyme.

February 23, 1946

WEDDING DAY
AUSTRIA
Short Story

Looking out the window every few minutes to see if it has stopped snowing, but I see that it is still coming down quite heavy. It looks so soft and so white, like the wedding dress laid out for the coming big day tomorrow. The big question is: will it stop snowing? If not, I might not get to wear it. It is very questionable if the three cars we have arranged for can make it out of our town and up the steep hill, without snow chains. Two of the three cars we know do not have them. How could we make it to the church, which was about three miles away? And if not, can the one car that has the chains get us there?

Tomorrow Joska will be my husband.

I am practicing that strange Hungarian name I will have, as I keep looking out the window. Joska and a friend are on their way to bring his bed from his place in Gmunden to our apartment in Theresienthal, where we are planning to live with my mother. She has a small extra room and we would be welcome there. Lucky us!! Remember, this is 1946, and it is impossible to find a place to rent or things to buy with money. It is an exchange/trade time for everything you need.

The morning is here, the snowfall slowed down, and here we are, how to fit six family members into a small car for four persons. Both of my sisters put on their snow boots and start walking the long way. With mom in the car, the snow chains on, Joska and I hope to make it up the steep hill. The last thing the chauffeur says is, "Put a shovel in the trunk, just in case." (It was a good thing, it came in handy in a difficult spot.)

Finally, we are at City Hall for the civil ceremony. One of our witnesses seems to either have forgotten where he is supposed to be, or, we are thinking he might have had an eventful night, and overslept. We wait quietly and patiently a bit, letting two other couples go ahead. But our nerves are being tested, not to lose the spirit of this day. Here he is, finally! and he does look like he had an eventful night. The formality in the City Hall does not take long and soon we are on our way to the church. That is another mile, but easy going, no hills, thank God, and the streets were somewhat cleared of the snow.

The church was built on a small island on Lake Traunsee around the 11th century, the lake is surrounded by mountains. Only by walking over a long 106 meter (approximately 360 ft.) bridge can you reach it. That is easily said. Today, on my wedding day, the bridge is under three to five feet of snow. I stand before it, in a long white dress.

Over my dress is a lace coat. Nothing, not even this snow and icy cold, can convince me to cover my beautiful dress. We are told that the bridge had been cleared of snow already three times this morning, for us.

My family and our friends are all there. The Priest, Father Aigner, who is performing the ceremony, was my catechism teacher for many years. When he gives us his blessing, I can feel his good prayers and his well wishes coming from his heart. I hold a special place there. Greti, the name he calls me now, is the name he has called me since I was 10 years old.

We are lucky that Joska has a friend who is a photographer, something that would have been almost impossible to find. The ceremony is over now, and we are leaving the church. Suddenly, on the bridge, two American Military Police are coming towards us and they arrest our photographer friend. They take his camera from him, and I think: there go all our wedding pictures.

When I go back to the events, the thought comes back too: what else can go wrong? We did not hear from him. We had no idea where they had taken him, or why. And we thought we never will.

Our whole family had been saving our meat ration coupons for two months before our wedding, and now we had enough to invite our closest friends to a restaurant for a late lunch. After the morning snowfall came a light drizzle, and then the sun came peeking through, showing us she wanted to be part of our day too.

My mother looked at us and said, "This marriage will last. You had snow, rain, and sunshine, all that heaven gives us." Was it to be that way? 57 years, mom, 57 years, and you were right, in your motherly wisdom, as always.

One year later, our photographer came visiting and brought us our pictures. They had been confiscated by the MP, and later returned with their apologies. It was all a mistake. He had been a Hungarian officer during the war and was investigated. He was cleared, and let go. Thank God they did not destroy the pictures.

Schloss Ort, Gmunden. The long walk over the snow-covered bridge. Ilona was baptized there, and later, on a trip to Austria, Michele was also baptized in Ort.

Schloss Ort courtyard showing the painted line where water levels were measured dating back to 1541.

Walking upstream from Theresienthal to Gmunden along the river Traun, on the right just before the brewery is where Joska proposed to me in 1945.

Honeymoon

GMUNDEN, AUSTRIA, 1946
Short Story

As I have said before, almost everything you needed or wanted was negotiable with cigarettes or food coupons. Taking that road, we found a nice hotel in Bad Aussee, about 30 miles south of Gmunden. It is a small mountain community with incredible surroundings. Mountains towering on all sides, wherever you looked. How lucky to find a room in this picture-perfect place that was covered with six to eight feet of snow.

It was about three or four hours after we had unpacked and explored the neighborhood when that nice room felt kind of cold. So I went down to the office and told them. The lady shook her head at me and I could not believe what I heard: "Sorry, ma'm the American soldiers moved out at midday and we are not permitted to heat the rooms for the public." We were shocked, shocked and very cold.

Overnight, the ice flowers on our room window were blooming…beautiful, but we just didn't need them to bloom on the 'inside' of the windows! The water in the room was like ice. Well, there was one warm and cozy place in the room. You guessed it! And we stayed there, snuggled, whenever we were not in a restaurant or sightseeing. The snow walls along the street from the street sweeper were 8-10 feet high. With the sun shining, it was truly a winter wonderland to see. If only we had a warm room to go home to.

But when you are in love, everything else takes second place. So in those five days we had a wonderful honeymoon and a good reason to snuggle up (as if we needed one). Thank goodness thick down beds kept us comfortable. The days flew by, and cold or not, we were on cloud nine.

After we came home we told our friends about the "Eis Hotel". The comments were not favorable toward our American occupiers! But it sure was a time to remember.

BAD AUSSEE Courtesy of Reinhard Hopperger www.BeautifulAustria.com

Hungary

A Trip Behind the Iron Curtain

HUNGARY
Short Story

It is now 1948. Our little girl is now two years old and coping quite well in two languages, in the limited vocabulary for this age. This was the time when we seriously considered leaving Austria. In a surprise move, the Hungarian Government, ruled by Russia, agreed to let Budapest have a World Fair…and issued visas for a short stay to Western Europe.

Joska had not spoken nor heard from his parents since he left without saying goodbye in 1944. They could receive our mail and knew what was happening in Joska's life, but there could be no mail out of Hungary. The men thought hard about taking advantage of the visa that was offered, Joska didn't trust the government, and it turned out he was right. He, of course, could also never risk to ask for a visa, he would never have made it back to us. But, what about me? Not a chance, with this Hungarian name I could not cross and return over the border. What if I go under my sister Resi's name, would it work? Well, she was 33 years old, and I was 25. We had pictures made of her for the passport wearing a sweater and earrings that I intended to wear. I would fix my hair the same way as hers in the picture, so, with a quick look, it could work.

I wanted to go to his homeland, bring back something that was meaningful for

My sister Resi's passport photo

him, and most important, meet his mom and dad, and three sisters. To this day I ask myself, why didn't anybody stop me?

And so it was that I found myself on the train, leaving Austria and approaching the Hungarian border. The train stopped and the border patrol asked for passports. He looked at the picture, and me, good thing that when the heart is going bump-a-dee-bump, it makes no sound. Well now, that was going as planned, I must say. When the train stopped in Budapest, I looked if I see somebody resembling Joska. Yes, three ladies, about three tracks away, were waving. Every four to five meters Russian soldiers stood with their guns crossed, determined to prevent people from doing what I was intending to do: coming and going with a false passport. It was frightening, as they showed me the way to reach the ladies.

As I reached them, I saw their questioning eyes eager to whisper the question, "Are you Greti?" You see, in our letters before the visit, it was always said that Resi, my sister, would visit, so nobody would get in trouble. My knowledge of the Hungarian language was more than limited, but we somehow, mixed with a little German, made it work. And if it didn't, nobody noticed. We had to take a different train to go about 20-

30 miles to a town called Alsogod, where Joska's parents were living. The train stopped, and there they were, Joska's parents. The greeting was just a little handshake, dad took my suitcase, and we walked to the house. Wow, I thought, that sure was not a receptions I was hoping to get. Oh my, what a greeting it was. But, as we entered the house, and the door was closed, dad took me in his arms, holding me, and all he would say is, "You are Greti, aren't you?" Now we really could let go with all the false pretenses. Why the cool reception at the train station? One word, 'fraud'. It would have given the truth away, that I was not the sister, by showing your emotions. After all, it was a small town and everyone knew each other. Or did they?

Dad spoke a good German dialect, like they speak it in Southern Germany. That is where his ancestors came from. Later they settled down in Siebenburgen, which at that time (1800) was part of Hungary. Dad and I could talk, and he could translate to mom and sisters. Sometimes in the middle of telling all they wanted to know, dad went around the house, checking if anybody outside was listening to our conversations. It really was an eerie feeling. "You see," he said, "in the next house lives a lady who is a strong Communist Party member." That night when I went to bed, Joska's mom sat by my bed like I was a little girl. She was telling me (I guessed) all the things about her little boy, thinking I understood it all. I never said I did not. I wished so much I could.

After staying a few days, dad got uneasy and he was afraid people would recognize me from the wedding photos that we sent in 1946 and they had shared with their neighbors. It was decided I should stay with Margit, the youngest sister, in Budapest, where I would blend in much better. By now, I wholeheartedly agreed. We said goodbye, packed a few things, sewing them into the lining of my coat. Joska's father's words were, "Take care of Dody, you got the best one of my children". Dody was the name they called him at home. It means 'little brother'.

After a somewhat easier time in Budapest, filled with sight seeing, I got back on the train to go west. Dressed as I was on the first trip, I shared a compartment with a Priest from Switzerland. "Oh my! Here comes the border patrol," the Priest said, "I hope they don't give me trouble, they don't like the religious people too much." Well, the border patrol made him open every bag, not missing a thing. My suitcase was up on top in the corner, and I think, after they finished with him, they got lazy, looked at my passport, and left.

We started to move again and I saw the sign on the other side of the border: AUSTRIA. The full impact hit me as we reached Vienna! The first phone call I made was to Joska's office, to tell him I have made it to Vienna. Nobody at that time had a phone in their homes.

The next stop to be was Gmunden. When I stepped off the train and saw Joska and Ilonka standing there, it was a picture that is etched in my mind. His face, when he saw me, told me all that I needed to know. The relief, it was written all over it.

Thinking back, only young people do something like that. How many times did we say that to each other over the years? If I can set aside the dangerous risks and see it as the experience it was. Was it worth it? Yes! Would I do it again if I could? NEVER, NEVER.

Note: Joska's three sisters are, in order of age: Elisabeth, Ilona, Margit. Joska was the third child...as I was too. We both had three girls and one boy in our family. His mother's name was also Ilona. Our Ilona's name is the third generation.

Joska (12) and his sisters.
(clockwise) Elizabeth,
Ilona, Margit

Joska's mother and father. Ilona Bolla Wagner, and Joseph Wagner. Both died before we became US citizens and Joska could go back without fear of not being allowed to leave again.

Ilona Bolla Wagner, 1885-1960

Joseph Wagner, 1882-1962

Argentina

A Little Girl's Easter Gift

ARGENTINA, 1949
Short Story

It was Saturday morning, I was up at 5:00 to do, as always, the laundry for the people in the big house, and there was lots of it. Joska was taking care of Ilonka in that little shack with the dirt floor that was in the back of the main house. It was just big enough to hold one bed. It was Easter Saturday, and he didn't have to go to work. Oh my, I was thinking, what an Easter this is. No Easter eggs, or anything, that we could do for Ilonka in this situation here.

As I was hanging the laundry on the clothesline, it really got to me. My face must have been not very good in hiding my feelings, as I felt something is pulling on my dress. As I looked down, there was a little face looking at me, as she was studying mine. A voice so tender said, *"Mami, ich hab dich so lieb"* (Mommy, I love you so much). All I could do was kneel there with her, holding her, saying the same thing to her, over and over.

How did she, and however will she know, the strength she gave me when I needed it most? It was as if the strength was coming back to me. Joska came and said, "Can you cook some eggs? I will color them, I have colored pencils." Yes, it worked, although the three eggs were white, but he was doing the best he could, and he saved Easter for Ilonka. Our first Easter in Argentina. I still see that little face, and these eggs, colored, and the love given to me to get through this hard time.

...And we did it together.

THEY'RE ONLY BANANAS

BUENOS AIRES, 1949
Short Story

    It must have been two or three weeks since we were living in that shack behind the main house where I was working as a maid. We were waiting for Joska to find work thru a friend, who promised him that he will find a place for him.

    Finally, Joska found work in a machine shop, and if all goes well, tomorrow he gets his first pay. In all this time we had no money whatsoever and could not buy anything we needed or wanted. This night, when I went to bed I could only think that tomorrow I can buy for the first time something that Ilonka has had to do without and watch the other little girl enjoy. How could she understand at such a young age, why I was handing this strange child something she loved, and did not give to her.

    It broke my heart many times a day.

    I could hardly wait for Joska to come home I was so excited, thinking I could buy some fruit for us when the *verdulero* man comes with all the vegetables and fruits on his daily stop here. I saw the grandma who lived with the family buying every day bananas and all other fruits. It was always just for them we could never have any. Ilonka and I just loved bananas, a rare fruit in Europe. So, when Joska came home and gave me the money there was one condition: "Tomorrow when the verdulero comes, you buy some bananas for Ilonka and you, promise?" This promise he knew would be kept!

The next morning, as the horse-drawn wagon with all the good stuff came, the lady of the house was there and finished her purchase. She was surprised to see me standing behind her and said something I could not understand to the man. I walked up to him and took about six or eight bananas and some apples. Grandma there got into the action fast, she was waiving her arms, frantically pointing at me and probably making clear to the man that she was not about to pay for the things I was holding in my hand. As I could not explain in words, I showed him and her the money and I paid for it with the first money Joska earned here.

Ilonka and I finally had our bananas. That afternoon, when I handed Ilonka a banana and said, "Eat as many as you want." That made my heart sing. We saved some for Joska, oh was he happy! Seeing the look on her little face assured me that the money could not have been spent in a more gratifying way. It made me feel so rich, and so good, to be able to get Ilonka what she so wanted.

….and these were only bananas, you would say.

JUST AN EVENING BATH

BUENOS AIRES, 1949
Short Story

We are now experiencing winter in Buenos Aires in our first rented house. It is not a winter we were accustomed to, coming from Austria. This was June/July, the Argentine winter months. The temperature during the day was about 60-70 degrees, and about 50 degrees during the night.

Joska was working in a machine shop across town and had to take the train. His working hours were stretching into late evening hours, until midnight. I was happy when my friend Elli came to visit. She came with us from Gmunden. Elli was only 16 years old when she got married to a friend of Joska's. Her mother in Gmunden made me promise that I look out for her a little bit...so I did a little of this.

It was bedtime for Ilonka, and she was ready for her bath. That meant heating the water outside on a coal burning small barbecue and filling a tin bathtub for the bath. Since the house had no gas or electric heating, and the evening air was too cool, we brought the barbecue in the house. After we put Ilonka in the bathtub and played with her, both of us sitting on the floor by her, we saw Ilonka was falling asleep, yawning over and over. We laughed because that was funny. I looked at my friend Elli, and saw that that she is starting to yawn too. "It is only 9:00, Elli, are you tired too?" "Ja, let's all go to bed," she said, "I don't know why I am all of a sudden so sleepy." By now I got Ilonka out of the tub, the beds were already made for all three of us to hop in, as I felt very tired and sleepy now too.

It was as if somebody told me what to do. I yelled at Elli, "Help me to get the coal stove out of the house, I think some of the coals are not red all the way through, that is why we are all so sleepy!" We took the stove out, wrapped Ilonka in a blanket. She was sound asleep. We woke her up and Elli and I took turns carrying her in the front yard until 12:00 at night. All the windows were open when Joska came home. We were still walking outside with the sleeping little girl. Now I know, would we have stayed in the house, Joska would have been too late to help us. It was 2:00 in the morning when we finally found it safe to go to bed. That was the first and last time a coal stove did go inside any of my homes.

For three days, Elli and I had headaches that no pill was able to help. But that was a small price to pay when the thought came back, again and again: What if……?

First Argentine Veal Roast

ROJAS, 1950
Short Story

This is the land of meat consumption, I learned fast. After the first year in Buenos Aires, we were living in the little town Rojas. Across the unpaved dirt street, was my butcher. I was watching people buying meat in quantities I never saw in all my life. As I was told, beefsteak for breakfast, lunch, and dinner, was the menu.

My little purchase for usually one steak got the butcher's attention. He finally got the nerve to ask me, "Who in the family eats the meat?" the answer: "Well, we all do" startled him truly. As I got to know him, I was asking him how come there is no veal. I never saw it. He explained to me that it is against the law to kill calves. So, I had my answer, and my hopes crashed to ever get a taste of it.

About a few weeks after our conversation, he waved at me from across the street to come. He handed me a package, and said, "Don't tell anybody that I gave you some veal!" I was so excited and got my wood stove going. Looking at the meat, I wondered why it was so wobbly and grey looking. I was not very experienced in cooking, and thought, "Well, a good heat in the oven will fix that" I was sure. 'Wishful thinking' comes to mind. After a couple of hours we were going to have a wonderful meal. My mouth was watering already. Now it has got to be done, it is almost two and a half hours later.

As I finally took it out and tried to put a knife in this still grey-looking blob, I could not believe what I saw. A grey liquid running out of it, looking so awful, and not smelling good, either. Oh was I disappointed! The next day when I told my butcher what happened, he said that the calf was still in the cows womb and not born when the cow was slaughtered. That was the meat he gave me. Well! That was my first and last attempt to even think about veal in Argentina. In the meantime, we will stick with the Argentine staple food: beef. All I can say is, I tried!!

Joska and Ilona in Rojas

Mountains Calling Me

CORDOBA, ARGENTINA, 1950-1951
Short Story

You can ride the train for hours and hours across Argentina, and all you see is the pampas…flat and endless, it seems.

One day, Ilona was playing with a friend, and when she came home she told me excitedly that she went on a mountain. I had to see that! I saw it alright, it was an elevated train track, about eight to ten feet high. All I could think was: this child will never see one here. This thought occupied me more than it should. But the Austrian girl in me was calling me after two and a half years of endless pampas. All around us was flat, there was nowhere to go to see mountains.

The *Freie Presse* (Free Press) was our German newspaper. Our Spanish was not yet good enough to catch all the news. I don't know what made me look in the advertising section that day, I had never, ever, before looked there. There was a wanted ad for a cook at a summer-camp in the Cordoba Mountain Resort, run by a German teacher, for about 30 kids. Well, I did some soul-searching, thinking: how hard can it be to cook for kids? But 30 to maybe more? I don't know! I barely, after two and a half years cooking for my little family felt comfortable doing it. Until we left Austria, my mother did all the cooking, as she was home and I was working in the office. But, what could it hurt if I just try…it won't kill them. So, I sent a letter to apply, never expecting an answer, as our town was 600 miles away from Buenos Aires, where she lived. I also never mentioned it to Joska, as I said, I did not expect a response.

It was a week later, on a Sunday, a special delivery letter came for me from Mrs. Sievers. She was asking me to come to Buenos Aires for an interview. NOW it was time to tell Joska what I did. After a long discussion, he agreed that I at least should go see her.

Thank God she did not say in her letter that she was looking for a cook, just that she was looking for someone to help with the children. If Joska had known what my real duty was to be, he would never have let us go. That I know for sure. He understood my longing for the mountains he learned to love in Austria. So, I took the train, and was on my way to my interview.

When I arrived in Buenos Aires, I had to take a bus to Olivas, about a half hour bus ride. I have never been good in finding streets, so I missed the stop by five blocks. Let me say this: LONG blocks, in high heels, are murder. When I finally found the house, limping more than walking, I thought this is going to be a very interesting interview. It was!! She said when she saw me, 'Just sit down' and she brought me a basin filled with water and said to put my feet in, and rest for a moment. So there I was, soaking my sore feet, while she interviewed me. She won my devotion from this moment on.

OH YES, I cooked for a LOT of people before…that, and all the right answers were flowing from my mouth, and to this day, I don't know how I got through it. She hired me, and I was on cloud nine. Later, after proving myself, she admitted she did not believe one word about my cooking experience. But she was so taken by my enthusiasm and positive answers and willingness. Years later we often laughed about this, a lot.

Now came the hard part, telling Joska that for two and a half months he has to be alone. That took a lot of understanding on his side, and let's be honest, a good portion of guts and luck on my side. When I got home, he was happy for me and Ilonka, and I was thankful he let us go. We sure could use the money to buy a few necessary things. Money was tight; after all, we started with nothing.

And so, we went. I will never forget the first soup I made. It was the quantities I was struggling with. I know how to cook, but what if I don't make enough? After all, one never knows how much kids eat, and they were of all ages. Until this day I don't understand, whatever I cooked, it was good, and it was always enough.

Finally, mountains, rocks, and a girl in lederhosen!

Oh my, the legs are a little too short.

Ilona was happy, she got to ride a horse, play with so many kids, got things to experience that she would never forget in her life.

After six weeks, Joska came to visit. It was on a Sunday and I was making *Palachintas* (large crepes rolled up with jam) for 30 kids. They had begged me and promised to entertain me with Wiener Waltzers on the accordion while I flipped the crepes. In my bathing suit I was cooking. His eyes would not believe what he was seeing: me in the kitchen, surrounded by four teenager girls entertaining me with music and singing. Well, he now knew what I was doing here. When he felt the atmosphere, and saw the friendships in the camp, like a big family, he understood. Joska was very pleased with what he saw.

I was a cook by day, a teenage companion in the evening, and a very close friend with Selma (Mrs. Sievers), a friendship that lasted for years afterwards. To see Ilona in these surroundings was worth all the work. She was the mountain girl from Austria, so was I. We came back the next year for an encore, I guess my cooking must have been

Our group of workers and their children in Cordoba.
(left corner) me, Ilona, and Selma Sievers.

satisfying for everyone.

It was a happy, hard-working time. Lots of singing and laughing. Sometimes scary with scorpions in our bathtub, snakes in the dormitory, and bugs coming too close for comfort. But all of it, a lifetime of memories for both.

We were all young there, and in these mountains we were at home.

Cordoba taxi, the only transportation there

SANTO DOMINGO

I Must Be Color Blind

SAN CRISTOBAL, DOMINICAN REPUBLIC, 1953
Short Story

Yes, there were a lot of 'getting used to's and adjusting to do on this island here. Not all bad, but the primitive had its ups and downs. Everybody working for the *Armeria* (armory) was from Europe, and white. Walk two blocks, and you see the majority of the native population, black and extremely poor, with lots of children.

We all had maids to help with the housework. The humidity and heat was sometimes unbearable, and the women worked for affordable salaries. Rosa was working for me. When I first saw her doing my laundry in the backyard, boiling the whites in an empty tin can over heap of burning coals, and smoking a pipe in her mouth, it really startled me. But it got done, and I didn't have to do it. I would not know how, in this situation.

It was after lunch, which is the main meal here, and everyone takes a siesta. So did I. Rosa called and said very quietly, "Señora, there is a girl at the door asking for work, but she is so black, you don't want her!" Well, I looked at Rosa, thinking, how much blacker can she be than Rosa? That I must see, and got up to see her. Well, I tried and was unable to see the difference between the two of them. I obviously missed something, but for Rosa's sake, I agreed. That gave me the first, but not the only episode where I learned that a little lighter color goes a long way among the islanders. We Europeans, among the native population for the first time, just could not see the difference.

A scene outside the city

A Promise Kept

SAN CRISTOBAL, DOMINICAN REPUBLIC
Short Story

It was 1957 now, and springtime in Santo Domingo. There was really not much difference between the seasons. It was summer for us all year round, yes, the temperature changed a little, but that was all it was. Now it has been one and a half years that we said "Auf Wiedersehen" to our little girl, when she left us to stay with my sister Resi, Trude, and my mother. Joska's promise to my mother as we left in 1949 on that cold winter day was:

"Oma, with the first money I can save, and I don't know how long it will take, I will send your daughter home to see you!"

These were his last words to her. I think that promise was haunting him for eight years. So when we finally managed to have saved enough for two one-way tickets to Austria, I

Going home for the first time. Timi and I boarding our ship.

was on my way with Timi. To get us back again, he had to save at least five months for our return tickets to Santo Domingo.

We boarded a passenger ship and said goodbye. That was not easy, I was filled with mixed emotion, leaving Joska alone….but looking forward to seeing Ilona and taking her home with me, and seeing my family. On board this big ship, Timi was very excited as long as we were on deck and he could look at the water. As soon as we were in the cabin he would say, "Mami, I want to go on the ship, you promised!" Needless to say, we made a lot of trips up to see the "ship". Inside the cabin it was just not a 'ship', it was just a room for him.

After 15 days on the ship, we finally saw the Italian coastline with snow-capped mountains. "Oh my, snow!" Europe had a late winter spell, we were told, and it was cold. Well, my wardrobe for the last eight years was totally out of place here. I was unable to even buy any suitable clothes for this much cooler weather. No store in Santo Domingo carried them. For Timi, I made some sweaters before leaving, so he was somewhat protected. We were all on deck ready to leave the ship, when we were told that the ship was under quarantine. A passenger was ill, and until they were sure what it was, no one was allowed off the ship. Here we all were now, on deck, no food, no drinks, in the cold, for the next 12 hours. Imagine all the adults trying their best to keep the hungry and bored children calm. Finally after the quarantine was lifted, we left to take the train in Genoa, Italy, it was so, so, cold. Poor Timi, the word cold was nothing he had ever experienced.

It was 4:00 in the morning when we arrived in Bozen to take a different train connection. Everything in the train station was closed and they would not open any rooms for us to wait in. We were so incredibly cold, and when I saw that a booth was offering coffee and hot chocolate, it was what we both needed. When I ordered the drinks and wanted to pay, the man could not change my $10 bill, and so he would not give us the drinks. Thank God a gentleman behind me took the cups and gave them to me and Timi, he paid for them. I reached in my purse and gave him a pack of Marlboro cigarettes. He was so thankful for the "American" cigarettes, and so were Timi and I, for the warm drinks. We came now to the last stage of our long journey and my excitement was growing by every mile behind us. Somehow the train did not go fast enough. My emotions were far ahead of it. Timi's "Are we there yet?" questions did not help either. But, the train was finally slowing down, and here it is, the sign saying: GMUNDEN!!!

As the train was slowing down, my eyes were searching for the little girl I put on a plane one and a half years ago. Oh my! There she was, right out of a picture book. A red-cheeked country girl with braids. So healthy looking that I could not believe this was the same child who left Santo Domingo. One thought was racing through my mind like a lightening that struck me…..it was the right decision we made one and a half years ago…this wiped all the previous thoughts and guilt away with what I saw and felt, by looking at that Austrian girl I was holding in my arms. Timi now had his sister back, looking closely at her to find her again in the way he remembered. It did not take long to find that connection.

When we arrived at my sister's house, there was mother. Almost in disbelief, as she saw me, her eyes could not hold the tears. And neither could mine. She looked me over and over and said: "Joska has held his word, I thank him for that."

I was home again. My eyes were hungry for the familiar sights. The mountains around our city were full with snow, like on a winters day, they looked like they put their best dress on just to greet me. That was a sight to take in after the very different landscapes we have lived through in the last eight years. But it was cold, I forgot that March can be like this.

Mom lived in one room, which was big. It was the kitchen, dining room, and bedroom, all in one, really cozy. She took me there, and for the next six months, that was my home too. She stayed with my sister, who was just about 400 yards away. The next day she showed me something. She opened her linen closet door, reached in between the neatly kept bed sheets, and handed me an envelope. My mother said to me, "From the day you left, I was putting every month aside some little money just for the day you would come, so I have something to give you." I just looked at her, and saw how proud she was that she could do this for me. "Go," she said, "and buy some warm clothes for you and Timi, and don't say no. I was living for this moment for the last eight years." Yes, I could see it, her face said it all. So, I went and bought warm clothes and long pants for Timi, among other necessary warm things. I found out from my sisters that they were trying to convince our mother that she should exchange her bed, which was old and worn out. She would not spend the money, she had better things to save up for. The bed was good enough for her. When I heard that, we ordered the new bed, and when she found out that I could still get the things she wanted to buy for me, she was happy with the new bed. For Timi we got a scooter, wide tires with inner tubes, and in no time he was known in our town as the 'little wild American driver', fearlessly flying down the hills around us. Thank goodness there were not many cars to stop him then. (They called him American because we lived in Central America…it was all America to them) The time went by fast. A lot of letters crossed the ocean. Nobody at this time had telephones, so letters were all we had to communicate by. I was always a good letter writer, Joska, well, let's just say he struggled to this tune that was never his passion. I think men are never good at this.

Summer came, and I hoped Joska has enough money saved to let us come back. It was the end of August, when he was able to do that. And let me tell you, there was just enough time, as I was told that the last ship to Santo Domingo leaves in September of this year. That was a close call. I was horrified, thinking we have to stay the winter. I want to see my Joska, and the warm sunny island!

And so it's good-bye again, but this time with the hope that we will be back again, and not to have to wait eight years. That made it easier. And thank goodness we did come back a few more times. But this first one was unmatched by all the following visits.

United States

Timi's Short First School Day

GARDENA, CALIFORNIA
Short Story

It is the end of February, 1959. Ilona is now at Gramercy School in Gardena. Another language to master, after German, Hungarian, and Spanish. But for her, she adapted well to school and liked it.

As September came, it was Timi's turn to enter school. Ilona took him on the first day with her. The children were playing on the playground, waiting for the bell to ring to go inside. The bell rang. Everybody now is going to their classroom, or are supposed to.

It was about 9:30 in the morning when I was looking out the window from our second story apartment, when I saw a policeman holding a little boy's hand, coming towards our building. That little boy, yes, it was Timi. What in God's name, what has he done?

I ran down and when the policeman heard Timi calling me 'mama', I guess he accepted that as identification. I could not speak one word of English.

When he left, I found out that Timi thought 'when I hear the bell ringing in school, it is time to go home'. When the school found out what happened they sent Ilona home to see if everything was OK. By then it was. Well, later, as I was told, the following happened: when Timi left the school, to come home, he got lost. So as he was crying, a lady saw him and called the police.

The policeman drove through the school's neighborhood thinking that Timi will recognize the house where he lives. Thank God he did! That was his first school day in the new homeland. I don't think he ever forgot it, and neither did I.

Tell Me the Truth Mom!

GARDENA, CALIFORNIA 1961
Short Story

This morning, as always, everybody got ready to either go to school, or to work. Joska was the first one to leave, as his work hours started early. Ilona had already left for school, she was now at Peary Jr. High School, and Timi, as we now call him, was taking a long time in the bathroom to get ready. I knocked on the bathroom door and opened it. Here he was, in front of the mirror, and very intensely looking at himself.
As I looked and asked, "Is something wrong, Timi?", I could see something is really occupying his mind. "Are you OK?" I asked, "You're not feeling well?" Finally he said, in a very hesitant voice, "Mom, do you think it is alright if I let people know that I am really black?"

I was tempted to laugh, as I thought he was making a joke. But looking at him and seeing his concerned expression, I knew that he was very serious about it. "What on earth makes you think that?" I asked. "Oh mom, you don't have to hide it. I know I was born in Santo Domingo, and all the kids there are black." It took a while to make that blond, white, little guy understand that the land where he was born had no hand in his creation. "Look at your dad and me, WE gave you your life, do you see that?" "Really mom, am I going to look like *Apu* when I'm grown up?" "I sure hope so, that would be his gift to you. He is a very handsome man."

A happy little boy, this morning, went to school. I wondered how long he has struggled with it before he found the courage to ask. And, how many times were we teasing him with that story? Too many, I'm afraid.

Note: *Timi* - Timi's Hungarian name Tivadar is abbreviated Tivi…when we came to the US, we could not call him that, especially after he came home from school asking, "Do you know what my name means?? It means TV." He became Timi. Later Timi learned that the English translation of his name is Theodore, and he became Ted.

Apu (pronounced awe-pooh with accent on the 'awe') is short for Apuka and means dad in Hungarian.

The islanders

LET ME TALK ABOUT MY MOTHER

My mother Theresia Parzer Stockhammer,
9-24-1893 to 6-30-1979 and her mother, Maria Parzer

Now that you have read my stories, I think it's only right that you should know why I dedicated my writing to my mother. I'd like you to know her as my sister Trude and I recall her.

The truth is that I don't know if any writing about her could do her justice, but I will at least attempt to bring her into your hearts as she always was and will be in her children's hearts.

Lets go back a little. When my grandmother, Maria, fell in love with the son of a well-to-do farmer, his parents were not pleased. They wanted him to help enlarge the farmland, which meant to marry another farmer's daughter. The second and very important issue also came into play. To find a future wife, she had to prove that she is capable of bearing children, so the land could be passed on to the family members only. For this reason it was quite accepted that the bride-to-be was carrying a child. However, my grandparents were not landowners, and the son was threatened that he would not inherit the farm should he marry this fabric-worker's daughter. As we know, he left my pregnant grandmother and chose the farm. It was 1893, when a little girl named Theresia was born. My grandmother was working in the factory and with the help of her parents was raising my mother for the first few years. I don't know exactly when my grandmother got married, but she did, and the family grew to seven children, three girls and four boys. My mother was never accepted by her stepfather, and was never allowed to forget she was not his.

Growing into a 19 year-old beautiful young woman, it was no wonder she fell in love with a young, handsome, and very outgoing young man named Heinrich. He was, I was told many times, a person who could light up a room with his presence. It was 1913 or 1914 and plans were made to get married. WWI started and he had to leave her to go to war. And so, my oldest sister Resi (Therese) was born November, 1914. I believe the next few years, my mother worked in Germany in a city called Traunstein, and grandma was taking care of Resi for that time. As the war ended, my father came home.

He had served on the Russian Front and had been held in camp. Finally, the postponed wedding took place, and mom gave birth to three more children.

I think, as you read the stories, you could feel the love and the commitment my mother gave to her children. Her life was her children, nothing else had room in her heart. When my father was taken away from us, she was 32 years old, and oh, such a beautiful young woman. Men did not exist for her, and it was surely not for lack of attention. She would never give any man the right to be a stepfather to her children. They were hers, and she knew the hardships she was facing by doing it all alone.

I gave you just a few samples of her goodness in some of the short stories so you can know her, but there is one story that I have to tell you that says it all. Unpredictable stories that only life can write, tested my mother's good heart: The stepfather who had never given her one good word when she was a little girl was now very ill and needed around-the-clock care. For a year she alone made his remaining time bearable. One day he looked at her, took her hand, and said, "Why are you so good to me, when I was never a father to you?" "That was long ago" she answered, "and I have it all forgotten." None of his children who lived close by had time for their father.

When I look back at her picture now, all I see is the love and goodness in her face, nothing else has room there. I hope that I came close to making you feel that you know her just a little bit as she was, always kind, never have I heard a loud word in anger coming over her lips, never ever, never a judgment. The people in our small community loved and respected her so much. She found the right and kind words for all situations in her life. Mom, I wish I could be like you.

My sister, her husband, our mother

A beautiful little cemetery on a hill in Gmunden. The people take beautiful care of their loved-one's graves.

Looking Back on My Writing

When I started looking back, I stayed away from the political atmosphere that we encountered because I wanted to tell the journeys that life has allowed me to experience. A journey that was full of excitement, hardships, and of all the love to share with my husband of 57 years, loving children, grandchildren, and great-grandchildren.

Most events, until we reached the US have taken place in countries that were governed by dictators.

Austria was taken over by Adolf Hitler in 1938, and that ended in 1945 at the end of WWII.

Argentina, the president was Juan Perón, also a dictator. We saw him in 1950 with Evita in the Plaza de Mayo, admired and cheered by thousands of his people. Later after he was exiled and living in Santo Domingo, we greeted him on his daily stroll on the beach near our house, and again sitting in front of us in a movie theater. It was hard to believe that such a powerful leader became so ordinary.

Santo Domingo was ruled by the dictator Rafael Leonidas Trujillo Molina, *Presidente y Padre de la Patria Nueva* (President and Father of the New Homeland). He was still in control there when we left the island for the US in December 1958.

I have visited both countries, Santo Domingo and Argentina, in the 1990's and I must say: On Santo Domingo, when I saw the condition this land is in, I came to think that some nations are not ready for democracy. It was unbelievable. The conditions we found under the new democratic, free, environment, were atrocious. The people there have electricity only a few hours a day, the children have no light in the evening to do their homework or read, the streets need repair and are filled with trash…our beautiful island. As for Argentina, things are freer, but if they are better can only be answered by the Argentine people themselves.

A Letter to My Children

Dear children, grandchildren, and great-grandchildren,

Writing my life's story for you has let me re-live the good and happy times, but also the times that tested our family's strength and love to the fullest.

It was some years ago when Ilona asked me to make a tape of my life for her for Christmas. So I started, and I was not happy with it. For the first time I heard my accent, which I thought I didn't have, and I could hear my nervousness coming through. So, I let it go for a long time, but by then, my two persistent kids kept asking me to continue telling what they thought was quite an eventful life. I started writing about it instead, and found it gave me the peace that the tape recorder couldn't give me. I discovered that I could put it much better in writing. No accent there, and I was at ease doing it whenever I felt the need to write.

Surprised at my joy to do it, I started one little story. My life came 'to' life with every stroke. Inspired by my daughter's belief that all the stories I was telling her over the years should not be lost, and that they would be of interest to the children to come, I finally gave the pencil the green light to give it a try. Without her help in my less-than-perfect spelling and correcting some sentences, which would have lost something in translation, I could not have done it. As you read the stories, you will find a sentence or a word that will make you pause and think it is an error, but Ilona insisted that at least a little of the 'Gretl-way-of-talking' had to be preserved.

Thank you, Ilona, for being my inspiration, my typist, and my editor.

When Tim was told that I was writing, he insisted that the typed pages belong in a book. He was determined to give it the proper cover, and that it should look like a published book.

Thank you, Timi, for thinking so highly of my writing, that you invested in your mom's book.

To all of you belonging to our family, the pages you are reading gives you a look back where part of your family members came from, and the road they took to get here. Add your story and pass it on to your children.

With love, Your Mom, Omi, Oma

November 5, 2005
Torrance, California

Vienna was in then paid to reach the intended locations. That triget many parents to send there children to small towns in the western + soutern parts of Austria, as some bombs fell in Vienna. So when the war ended and Austria was divided among the 4 occupiers, the children could not go back to Vienna for quiet some time. Nobode was allowed to cross the Russian occupied eastern part in nich Vienna was. The Mailservice was not working across this Zones so good eather.

My Friend Emma, a Lady who came from Vienna a couple a year ago to work in Gmunden did find out, that her Neffew from Vienna was one of this children.

He was about 25 miles from Gmunden, in a small village Bad Aussee, staying with a Family. The Parant have not heard from him in the last few months and

Made in the USA
San Bernardino, CA
09 October 2017